PENGUIN BOOKS

IT IS WELL WITH MY SOUL

ELLA MAE CHEEKS JOHNSON was born in 1904 in Dallas, Texas. In 1924, she saw W. E. B. Du Bois speak at Fisk University, and in 2009, she attended Barack Obama's presidential inauguration in Washington, D.C. She is a great-grandmother and lives in Cleveland, Ohio.

PATRICIA MULCAHY is a freelance editor and writer who has worked on books including *Q: The Autobiography of Quincy Jones*, *Ten Minutes from Normal*, and *A Freewheelin' Time*. She lives in New York City.

IT IS WELL WITH MY SOUL

THE EXTRAORDINARY LIFE OF
A 106-YEAR-OLD WOMAN

ELLA MAE CHEEKS JOHNSON

with

PATRICIA MULCAHY

PENGUIN BOOKS

PENGUIN BOOKS
Published by the Penguin Group
Penguin Group (USA) Inc., 375 Hudson Street, New York, New York 10014, U.S.A. •
Penguin Group (Canada), 90 Eglinton Avenue East, Suite 700, Toronto, Ontario, Canada
M4P 2Y3 (a division of Pearson Penguin Canada Inc.) • Penguin Books Ltd, 80 Strand,
London WC2R 0RL, England • Penguin Ireland, 25 St Stephen's Green, Dublin 2, Ireland
(a division of Penguin Books Ltd) • Penguin Group (Australia), 250 Camberwell Road, Cam-
berwell, Victoria 3124, Australia (a division of Pearson Australia Group Pty Ltd) • Penguin
Books India Pvt Ltd, 11 Community Centre, Panchsheel Park, New Delhi – 110 017, India •
Penguin Group (NZ), 67 Apollo Drive, Rosedale, North Shore 0632, New Zealand (a division
of Pearson New Zealand Ltd) • Penguin Books (South Africa) (Pty) Ltd, 24 Sturdee
Avenue, Rosebank, Johannesburg 2196, South Africa

Penguin Books Ltd, Registered Offices:
80 Strand, London WC2R 0RL, England

First published in Penguin Books 2010

1 3 5 7 9 10 8 6 4 2

LIBRARY OF CONGRESS CATALOGING IN PUBLICATION DATA
Johnson, Ella Mae Cheeks, 1904–
It is well with my soul : the extraordinary life of a 106-year-old woman /
Ella Mae Cheeks Johnson with Patricia Mulcahy.
p. cm.
ISBN 978-0-14-311744-5
1. Johnson, Ella Mae Cheeks, 1904– 2. Johnson, Ella Mae Cheeks, 1904—Philosophy.
3. African Americans—Biography. 4. African American women—Biography.
5. Centenarians—United States—Biography. 6. Older women—United States—Biography.
I. Mulcahy, Patricia. II. Title.
E185.97.J(Johnson) A3+
305.48'896073—dc22
[B]   2009050161

Printed in the United States of America
Set in Simoncini Garamond • Designed by Elke Sigal

Penguin is committed to publishing works of quality and integrity.
In that spirit, we are proud to offer this book to our readers;
however, the story, the experiences, and the words
are the author's alone.

In memory of Tennie and Moody Davis, who raised me; for they began the story of my life and through their kindness taught me compassion.

In memory of my first husband, Elmer Cheeks, the love of my life and father of our adored sons, Jim and Paul.

To my two sons, for inspiring me and giving me strength as a young mother to carry on, and for continuing to love and encourage me; for my beloved grandchildren, Audrey, George, and Jimmy, who bring me great joy; and for my cherished great-grandchildren, Nika, Andrew, Alex, and Nico, who light up my life.

He hath showed thee, O man, what is good, and what doth the Lord require of thee but to do justly, and to love mercy, and to walk humbly with thy God.

—MICAH 6:8

CONTENTS

"A CHEERFUL GIVER BE"

WORKING WITH ELLA MAE

Frequently I get lost, in more ways than one. Driving to see Ella Mae Cheeks Johnson for the first time at Judson Park in Cleveland, I twisted and turned along the leafy road of the Ambler Heights Historic District near Case Western Reserve University, but kept missing the entrance to the retirement facility, discreetly marked with a small sign on a curvy road lined with old stone houses set back from the street, many behind near-walls of foliage. After a quick cell phone conference with Ella Mae's dear friend Betty Miller, I finally arrived to find the lady herself waiting to greet me in the lobby, wearing a pink dress and large dark glasses. Betty, an attractive, jovial woman dressed in resort wear and dangly earrings, was also sporting big shades as she pushed Ella Mae's wheelchair through the halls. Though warm and welcoming, these ladies were not fooling around: even a quick intro-duction told me that. They are can-do people.

Later I told Ella Mae Cheeks Johnson, then age 105, that she was the only person over 80 I'd ever met who never referred to her physical infirmities or health prob-lems. To which she replied, "I have my difficulties; I do not rejoice in them."

And why would she, when she has plenty of better things to think and talk about, and to reflect upon?

I knew Ella Mae was a reflective person even from our ten-minute phone conversation, which was how we met after an editor from Penguin called and asked if I'd be interested in working with a 105-year-old African American woman who'd come to his attention from in-terviews on National Public Radio and PBS at President Obama's inauguration. On the phone, Ella Mae was thoughtful and full of insight, utterly lacking in senti-mental platitudes.

Ella Mae Cheeks Johnson looks around and forward, every day. I told the editor I'd be glad to give it a try.

From day one of our taping sessions, I knew we were on the right track. She started out not by telling me where and when she was born, but that she defines her-self as "an unabashed beggar." A provocative statement!

Indeed, compassionate giving and aiding others is her lifelong mission. Outside the door to her room at Judson is a flower-bedecked sign that encourages all who enter: A Cheerful Giver Be.

Often during our interviews I'd ask after several hours had flown by, "Ella Mae, should we stop for a break?"

"Not necessarily," was the answer.

This is Ella Mae's way: if you'd like to stop, go right ahead. She won't tell you to stop because *she* needs to; nor will she say anything along the lines of, "Don't mind me." Even a simple exchange has nuance. Above all, she will not ask you for any special considerations because she is 106 years old. Her age is not beside the point; but it may not be the main thing, either.

Thus this woman, who was orphaned at age four and survived the Great Depression; lived under Jim Crow laws in the South; lost her beloved husband and raised two young boys on her own while being employed full-time as a social worker; and has kept up with active fund-raising and community affairs as a resident of a retirement community for thirty-four years, has a few things to tell us all about all-American grit, self-reliance, and independent thinking—not to mention the increasingly important virtues of adopting a cosmopolitan perspective.

She says she is a seeker. So here's some of what we found together, along with her wonderfully supportive friends, Betty Miller and Kathryn Karipides, without whom the project would not have gone as smoothly.

Most of all, listening to Ella Mae is fun, not merely inspiring and instructive; I can only hope I've done justice to that fact in trying to capture her voice on the page.

Being with her is fun, too. The first night of my initial visit, Rob Lucarelli, Judson's personable and efficient director of public relations, arranged for all of us to go to a local restaurant for a dinner celebrating the commencement of the book project. As we sat and contemplated salads or pasta dishes, Ella Mae wheeled up to the table and ordered lobster, followed by a large piece of cheesecake smothered with fruit for dessert. At age 106, she doesn't do things halfheartedly. Her flair for living comes through loud and clear, no matter what her age or immediate circumstances.

—*Patricia Mulcahy*
Jackson Heights, New York
Winter 2010

I know all this will not explain who I am and what I hope to do with my life. I simply hope this story will give you a glimpse into how I've lived—and my philosophy as a seeker.

I've had to speculate here and there about some details, given that I was born at a time when there were no official records in America for people of African descent. Nonetheless, I have tried to tell the truth of my 106 years on earth, as it is known to me. I am trying to show what I've lived through, what I've done, and what I've had to do without.

I am not saying I know everything. I am not saying nobody knows but me. I can only tell you what I know, the best way I can. Some of the things in this book happened over a hundred years ago. There are some things I recall, of which I can say, "Yes, I know this."

In regard to others, I've had to guess. I can't put a time or a name on everything. I never anticipated having to remember all this. I try.

Maybe my guess is wrong—but that's the way it is.

ACKNOWLEDGMENTS

To my family, who continue to be a source of love: the family of my late husband, Raymond Johnson; my daughters-in-law Mary Grace Concannon and Sandy Cheeks; Jenny Cheeks, mother of my grandsons, George and Jimmy; Wendy Gutierrez Cheeks, granddaughter-in-law; Dorothy Cheeks; and Nancy Stokes and family.

To the friends who through the years have given of their time and resources to support my many charities, I honor you. And to my friends who have known me over the years, I am thankful for your friendship and love. My gang, Dorothy Adams, Carol Henderson, Kathryn Karipides, Jean Kincaid, Joanna McLendon, and Betty Miller, are always there for me, and do much of the planning for my big birthday parties that raise money for charities such as HIV/AIDS, Kenya; Heifer International; and

Smile Train. Let the friends continue: Ruth Bonner, David Brown, Dr. Robert Beck, Mo Miller, Ethel Pye, Fedalma Drewery, Marjorie Turner, Theo Jones, Olivia Williams, Lavert Stuart, Raymond and Georgia Franklin, the Reverend Richard Andrews, Sr. (dec.) and his wife, Marjorie (dec.), Hugh & Marilyn Burtner, Dr. Edwin Eigner, Carol Adrine, Faye Jones Harrison, Rose Eaton, Leroy and Lois Roberts, William and Monica Reese, Lauren Reese, Scott Salaam, Peggy Page, Carl Bradford, Mark Bradford, Valerie Samuel and family, Theo and Angela Fielding, Ivan Foster and family, Cindy Kaprosky, Christine Kaprosky, Rayette Burks, William and Mary Boyd, Pallie Hunter (dec.) and family, and Dr. F. Allison Phillips, a former pastor at Mt. Zion, and his wife, Velma, who have attended my many birthday celebrations and have eaten lots of cake.

To the members and friends of Mt. Zion Congregational Church, UCC, where I worked and worshiped for eighty-three years: Pastor Paul H. Sadler Sr. and his wife, Kim, George and Cassie Ellis, Shirley Sacks, Nate and Marguerite Parries, William and Juanita Robinson, Calvin Merchant, Marian Laisure, Charlie Miller, Don and Betty Howard, Franklin and Hellen McCord, Doris Brooks,

Louise Billingslea, Ruth Browder, Mary Banks, Alice Taliaferro, Melissa Lewis, Al and Melba Bellmar, Dr. James and Lesora Greene, George and Bessie Grant, and Owen and Marina Grant.

To my dear and devoted Alpha Kappa Alpha Sorority, Inc., and the local Cleveland chapter, Alpha Omega members, I commend you for your vision, leadership, and service on the local, state, national, and international levels. I am honored to be a part of it. I will always cherish my outstanding service award presented at the 2006 Boule (AKA's national convention, held every two years). And to my many sorors, of whom I'm only able to list a few: Dr. Joan Baker, Ebraska Caesor, Joyce Thornton, Dr. Bertrice Wood, Sarafrances Wood, Annette Hamilton, Alvernice Blandon, Betty Snipes, and Dr. Zelma George (dec.). Thank you!

To Judson at University Circle, which I have called home for the last thirty-four years, special thanks and appreciation to the administration and staff: Cynthia Dunn, CEO; Dr. Elizabeth O'Toole, my physician; and Rob Lucarelli, Director of Communications, who helped to start me on my inauguration trip and adventurous book journey. And of course the loving and caring nursing staff at Gardenview, who continue to add quality and substance to my life. I am forever grateful.

Thanks to the Honorable Sherrod Brown, Ohio senator, for graciously providing "the winning tickets" for me to attend the inauguration of President Barack Obama with Judson nurse Iris Williams; and to the Honorable Louis Stokes, retired congressman, Eleventh District, Ohio, for your invaluable friendship through the years. Thanks also to Hazel O'Leary, president, Fisk University, my alma mater, class of 1925; to Cleveland mayor Frank G. Jackson, who honored me with a proclamation on my 103rd birthday, and to the Honorable Stephanie Tubbs Jones (dec.), who recognized my 100th birthday. Lastly, thanks to Grover G. Gilmore, dean, Mandel School of Applied Social Sciences, Case Western Reserve University, my alma mater, class of 1928.

Special thanks to the crew who enabled me to see my story in print: the staff at Penguin, including publisher Kathryn Court; associate publisher and editor in chief Stephen Morrison and his assistant, Emily Baker; assistant editor Rebecca Hunt; production editor Kate

Griggs; cover designer Margaret Payette; art director
Paul Buckley; and writer Patricia Mulcahy, who helped
me translate 106 years of life into a succinct storyline.
Very special thanks once again to my dear friends Betty
Miller and Kathryn Karipides, who were there to help
every step of the way in the preparation of this book.

CHAPTER ONE

Unabashed Beggar

She stretched out her hand to the poor.
Yea, she reacheth forth her hands to the needy.

—Proverbs 31:20

I have been a beggar, and I'm not ashamed of it—call me an unabashed beggar. All my life others have helped me meet my needs. Now I seek nothing but to be a Good Samaritan. Instead of depending on someone else, my goal is to help others who are needy—and I don't mean strictly in a financial sense. I don't use the term "to give back," because I seek not to give back but to remember, and to do something for the needy.

Sometimes people say "the poor." I don't say just "the poor," I say "needy," because a lot of people are not really needy in a financial way. They need affection—we all do. And we need to feel that we matter. I had, and have had, the good fortune to be helped when I needed it.

I was born in Dallas, Texas, on January 13, 1904, as

Ella Mae Smith. In those days, black citizens had no official papers—there was no proof that I was born. Years later, attention was brought to the matter when I wanted to travel and needed a passport, for which a birth certificate was required. I didn't have one. From the government's perspective, it wasn't important whether I was born, or when—on such-and-such a day at such-and-such time.

As the need appeared, I "made do" with whatever was available. I could use an old insurance policy, if it had my birth date on it. I could use case records or whatever records guaranteed my age.

Our people, we didn't go to court. I wrote to an uncle named Raymond who was about eight years older than me and described the situation. He said what he knew I wanted: but in truth he had no reason to be informed of when I was born. Nonetheless, I am sure Raymond was honest. And he wanted to help me, besides. It was this combination of records—or the lack of them—that permitted me to travel all over the world later on.

You have to understand that we're living at *this* time, and that was *that* time, when the government didn't record our vital statistics. Since there was nothing there, you had to speculate. This is a lesson, not for me, but for those who came thereafter: this is now, and that was then. If we didn't have the facts about our lives, we had to guess the best we could. Some things were possible, and others just were not.

My mother's name was Annie Dawson. My grandparents later told me she was nineteen when I was born. Though I have little memory of her, they said she was a very beautiful young woman. My mother was black, though I didn't know what that meant. I didn't know her. I didn't know what "white" meant, either. I never met my father, Matt Smith, or knew any members of his family. But I had to get that "Smith" from somewhere! My parents were human beings who had something to give to the world, however little it was.

As time passed, I decided all this wasn't as important as what I could contribute, in my way.

One day when I was four years old, I was standing outside our house when I noticed that the curtains had been closed. My mother was dead, of what we now call tuberculosis. My family didn't say so then, because infectious diseases were greatly feared. I was no longer anybody's child. I did know my mother's family—my grandmother Betty Beard and her husband, James Beard, children of former slaves, and their kin. Betty had three daughters; my mother, Annie, was the oldest. Two of the others were named Lula Mae and Lena. There were also two sons, Seay and Raymond.

But my grandparents couldn't support an additional person. So the next-door neighbors, named Davis, decided they would take me into their home and their hearts, and from then on I was their daughter. They embraced me as their own. Their two grown children no longer lived with them. Sometimes the Davis sons dropped in, to stay ten minutes or through dinner; but they didn't have a major role in my upbringing. I don't remember a time when I was special at the Davises; but there was no time when I wasn't. I was just comfortable.

Moody and Tennie Davis were my "mama and papa" until Tennie Davis died in 1923. I suspected that Tennie's name came from her home state of Tennessee—just a guess. As I've said, there was no official way to know these things. I never asked Mrs. Davis where her name came from. It didn't interest me: it was just who she was.

I believe the Davises were both children of slaves,

but that's just conjecture. If they didn't keep records in say, 1900, where in the world are we going to get information about who was born a slave and who wasn't? The Davises never had one day in public school, in formal education. They did the best they could describing or understanding their background and their place in the world; but they could only go so far.

I didn't learn much after 1904 about who I was: What child knows the people he or she is formed by? Or who she is, and who she wants to be? But when I was in need, I needed a home, I needed a family, and I needed people who cared. I needed people who would teach me by example more than by words—and as I went along, that's who I became.

Neither Mama nor Papa could read or write but Papa made a living as a butcher. I was as much at home in the Davises' home as I'd been in my mother's house because the two families had grown so close, living side by side.

I went to the Davises' with a few toys and my few dresses. Their house had two bedrooms, one for them and one for me. There was a living-dining room. No toilet, no running water, and no electricity—kerosene lamps provided light.

We took baths in the kitchen with water heated on an iron stove fired by wood, which was in the yard, also the site of the communal laundry. That's where people did laundry in the summer in a big iron pot. If we wanted to be sure the white clothes and linens remained white, instead of getting kind of grayish, this was the way we had to do it. We didn't regret it. We didn't know anything more! The privy was in the yard, as well. In the winter, we heated food and water and whatever we needed on a wood stove in the kitchen. We didn't go outside then to heat water for a bath.

I couldn't say, "I don't want to bathe in the kitchen." That didn't mean that the Davises kept me ignorant; it just meant the atmosphere was such that I didn't know there were alternatives until I'd grown.

At that time, many people were unemployed. They "made do." If I needed black shoes and I had white ones, someone got black shoe polish, and we colored them. If a garment was too long, we shortened it.

Mrs. Davis went out on day jobs as a domestic worker. One night she did not come back as early as I thought she should have to start Papa's dinner. I was about five at the time. I took a lot of flour and water, and as I was mixing it, Mr. Davis came in and asked, "*What* are you doing?"

I said, "Mama isn't here, she didn't get ready for your supper (we called it 'supper' then), so I'm preparing it." At this point flour and water were all over the place.

Mr. Davis turned to me and said, "Come here. I'll help you clean up. If your mama gets here and sees what you've done, she'll kill you."

That, of course, wouldn't be true. But he was emphasizing what he considered important. I didn't make the bread.

The Davises were good people. They were kind. They didn't struggle for things for themselves; they gave me what I needed. I was never hungry. I liked greens: green vegetables, green tomatoes, or green beans. Beans were a major part of our diet—red beans as well as green ones, and peas. We liked baked beans. But they didn't come out just as beans: they were a meal, cooked and seasoned with bacon or ham. Much of what we ate came from Mrs. Davis's garden: beans, peas, greens, okra, yams, and sweet potatoes. See, there's a difference between yams and sweet potatoes. Sweet potatoes are a lighter color. I didn't like them as well as I did the darker ones. I needed pepper sauce to spark them up, and add zest.

Mama raised chickens and made corn muffins, too. She was skilled at "making do." Sometimes we bought watermelon from a man who came around on a wagon. We "plunked" the melon with a crooked finger to see if it was ripe or not. This would be primarily in the summer or the spring. In the winter, we went to the grocery stores. Mama canned fruits and vegetables and put them away for the colder times. I did, too, once I was grown.

There were very few professional people in our neighborhood, just hardworking people trying to make ends meet. But I never felt I needed clothing Mama and Papa couldn't buy for me. That's the way they managed. Everything in the Davis environment left me certain I was loved.

I remember Papa taking me in a cart one day as he raced his horse in a rural area. A neighbor asked if I was afraid and my response was, "No, Papa won't let me get hurt." But I also saw that some things were out of Papa's control. At that time in Dallas, if the police wanted to come into your house, they just did. They kicked the door in. They didn't wait to be admitted. If they were trying to find someone, they assumed all blacks, or Negroes, or colored people, or whatever they called us, knew all the others of our race.

Papa said, "I don't know where he is; I don't know where he lives." They swore at him and threatened him with physical violence. Whether or not Papa knew where this person was, he wouldn't say. Lying was the only protection, so that other people wouldn't be exposed. A lot of people lied. But who's to criticize them? They had to lie in order to survive.

When I saw my father so embarrassed and so humiliated and so helpless, I thought, "He can't help me, he can't protect me—he can't even protect himself." I know that was what the policeman wanted to convey, with his threats. He knew we were helpless.

I entered elementary school when I was five years old. I walked to school each day, making friends along the way. Our school was segregated, with all black teachers. Every day I came home for lunch. The Davises were caring parents. The only time I remember Mama being stern with me was when one of my classmates in what we now call middle school got into trouble with a boy. Mama told me, "If I ever hear that about you, I'll take you to school spanking you all the way. And then once we get there, I'll spank you some more, to show all the class what you've done."

I never wanted to give her reason to carry out this threat, but I never believed she would. She might have made me stay in. Remember, I wasn't born at a time when parents consulted a book, like Dr. Spock. The Davises and other parents would use such expressions to impress a child. They wouldn't literally carry out all the threats. They just wanted to put a little scare in me to show me the way. When Mama emphasized that if I got into trouble she'd spank me all the way to school, and keep it up once we got there, she was using the thought of public humiliation as the main deterrent.

Mama didn't have to beat me to show me what to do. It was important to me not just to please her but also to have her feel comfortable with what I did, and not be embarrassed by my behavior in any way. It was up to me to straighten up and fly right!

I remember one teacher from middle school in particular, Miss Jones, because she was dependable and had high expectations of her students. But she didn't browbeat us. She was slender and slow moving, and very neat.

In the senior class at Dallas Colored High School, there were many Maes: Lula Mae, Susie Mae, Minnie Mae, and others. I can't tell you why. It was just done that way then. I suppose that in some families there might have been more than one Mae: a mother or an aunt as well as a child with the name. Maybe they put another name in front so you could distinguish between the two.

There came a time when I was in my teens that I didn't want to be named Ella Mae. There were too many others. So I announced to my family and friends that I was going to be Ella Marie. I never heard a thing about it. No one ever called me Marie.

There were many ways in which we were put in our place in the Jim Crow South in which I grew up. Laws decreeing segregation of the races in all public places had been put into effect throughout the South after Reconstruction in the 1870s. The phrase "Jim Crow" came from a song called "Jump Jim Crow," performed in a minstrel show by a white actor in blackface. I had to sit in the balcony in movie theaters. Because of limited funds and prejudice, public facilities were denied me, including public transportation, swimming pools, restaurants, and most hurtfully, libraries. The last was my greatest loss. At Dallas Colored High School, most students borrowed each other's books.

I did well in high school due to the efforts of teachers like Mrs. Frazier, who was precise and didn't stand for foolishness. I was salutatorian of my graduating class. The valedictorian was Helen Tyler, my best friend all through high school. We didn't have a rivalry; each of us did the best she could. But I think I must have been better at math than she was. And she was better at English. Helen was without parents, but she had two maiden aunts who were schoolteachers, and they helped her. Even with no man in the home, they had a nice home materially, and got along with people. In those days, there were plenty of other students who didn't live with their biological parents. They were taken in by relatives or neighbors. There was no court to take care of it.

Helen went on to attend Howard University, and over the years we stayed in touch. I visited her and her husband once in Silver Springs, Maryland.

On weekends in Dallas, I attended church services at CME (Colored Methodist Episcopal) with my maternal grandparents, who lived about fifteen blocks away from the Davis home. On Saturday evening, I'd go over there in order to attend church with them the following day.

Mrs. Davis didn't interfere with that. My grandmother was ahead of her time, because people then criticized young congregation members for dancing. One day my grandmother said, "You can dance in my house," which meant the children could dance with me or her children at *her* house, even if they lived somewhere where their parents wouldn't allow it. She was uneducated and illiterate, but she knew her own mind. She wasn't perfect. She didn't try to be. She just lived and taught the best she could.

I participated in youth programs at CME. In fact, I was so active at the church that Mama once said to me, hoping I'd slow down, "The doors will open one day without you." They did! The service managed to go on even when I wasn't in attendance. I wanted to be connected with a church, even though I didn't know what it meant. There were just things going on there that I liked. I went to church school, what we called Sunday school. I taught in Sunday school, too. But nobody trained me. I studied the Scriptures at such a young age. We didn't have books. We had cards with stories on them, and pictures of the Prophets, and references to the poor. So that's the way I grew and learned.

Mrs. Davis was a Baptist. But she never said, "You've

got to go to my Baptist church," when I was going with my maternal relatives to Methodist Episcopal. I was shown early on that there is a difference between expressing a view or adhering to a faith, and saying "my view or no view."

Mr. Davis was not a churchgoer. One day Mrs. Davis's pastor came to see her, but she wasn't dressed. Mama had to go up and comb her hair. While she was gone, the minister started talking to Mr. Davis. Among other things, he said, "You should give to the church," and the implication was money.

Mr. Davis said, "Let's think about that. You're younger than I am, aren't you?"

The pastor said, "Yes."

So Mr. Davis said, "Will we take for granted I'll die before you?"

To which the pastor said yes again.

Mr. Davis concluded, "Then I'll take the money to Him myself."

After that the pastor didn't have a lot to say.

Tennie Davis was an unsophisticated person who did not require material things in order to value herself. She practiced her religion every day, teaching me that God created everyone in His image, and that I should respect all as I respected Him. She said that gossip should be avoided because it was usually about someone's pain or problems. And I should never blame other people for my own problems or disappointments. In fact, even when I knew I was not responsible, I need not put the responsibility elsewhere.

I have always tried to live by Mama's lessons. I attended CME until I left home to study at Fisk University, a historically black college in Nashville, Tennessee, in 1921. One of the administrators at the Dallas Colored High School, Mrs. Morgan, was a Fisk alumna and a former member of what was called the Fisk Glee Club. As my music teacher and a fellow member of CME, where she'd heard me sing solos with the church choir, she knew I had a flair for music. So she persuaded the rest of the Dallas alumni to help send me to Fisk, which was well known for its music programs. They made the arrangements and I went. What they wanted to do was pay for my music lessons and classes and so on; but I needed shelter and tuition—all the basics. They did not let me down. They gave concerts and raised money in other ways to fund my first year at the college.

At this point in my life, I was ready to go on to the next thing. There was so much future to look forward to.

If I was in a class and made a mistake, I hoped my teacher would explain what I'd done wrong, so I wouldn't make the same mistake the next time. I didn't think it would be helpful for me just to be told, "This isn't correct." I wanted to know why. At 106, I still want to learn from my mistakes.

CHAPTER TWO

COLLEGE GIRL

Education is that whole system of human training
within and without the school house walls,
which molds and develops men.

—W. E. B. Du Bois

Sit down servant,
I can't sit down

—Traditional spiritual

Because neither the Davises nor my relatives could help me with college costs, I had to rely on scholarships, fellowships, and my earnings on and off campus. At Fisk, they had someone on staff who looked for places to get scholarships and find jobs for needy students. That's what they did for the remaining three years I was there. Scholarships were secured for me, as well as work. I worked in the dining room and other places on campus, and at the YMCA and YWCA in town. When I was not in school, and during the summer, I worked, too. I had little or no free time.

At the YWCA, I was a waitress in a ladies' tearoom. At the YMCA, the menus were aimed at pleasing everyone; it wasn't just for the people who lived there. If you were going downtown and wanted to eat, you'd drop in.

Our clientele was integrated but the workforce was not. One summer I served fifteen gallons of ice cream a day. I couldn't eat ice cream for years after that.

After I left Dallas for school in Nashville, I never saw Mama again. She died during my sophomore year, and there were no funds for me to go to Texas for the funeral. I was greatly saddened by her death. Right before I left for school, we'd had a talk in which she confided that she'd always been afraid I would leave and go back to "my family," by which she meant my mother's kin. At the time, I thought how sad it was that Mama didn't seem to realize she *was* my family.

I knew how lucky I was to be at Fisk, founded barely six months after the end of the Civil War to educate freed slaves. It was one of many historically black colleges established then. By the turn of the century, there were seventy-seven of them nationwide. Most of the first students shared a common experience of poverty and slavery; nevertheless, they possessed a great thirst for learning. Slaves had been denied education on threat of corporal punishment. Americans of African descent flocked to Fisk and other schools to get the tools to survive. By the time I got to Fisk, it had evolved into a well-respected seat of higher education. Classes were held in a former Union Army barracks near the present site of Nashville's Union Station.

Because I had a good singing voice, my music teacher brought me to the attention of Fisk's renowned troupe the Jubilee Singers, who performed traditional spirituals, then called "slave songs," such as "Go Down, Moses." The first singers started as a group of traveling students who set out from Nashville in 1871 to raise money to keep the school open. Fisk literally sang itself into permanence. Though the Singers struggled at first, soon they were performing for audiences that included General Ulysses S. Grant, Mark Twain, and even Queen Victoria. Given that the Singers had contributed mightily to the school's continuance over the years, it seemed fitting that I arrived there on the equivalent of a music scholarship.

There were some people who didn't want to sing these "slave songs." But we believed what we believed. The songs inspired us to go in a special direction. It was because of the Jubilee songs, or spirituals, that I decided to go to the Holy Land years later. My spiritual life began in the choir at Fisk. Though we sang spirituals, I wasn't part of the actual Jubilee Singers troupe, but of the Fisk Glee Club and Chapel Choir. Spirituals influenced what became my life's mission, reminding me of the sufferings of enslaved people in Egypt and in the United States, too.

When I went on to college, I had to take remedial reading. I borrowed books right, left, and center from the college and public libraries and later bought them with the money I earned. As a result, I have a lifelong and passionate commitment to the written word. I majored in French, which I did not plan to study initially. But I needed one year of a Romance language, so I decided to sit in on a French class taught by Madame Shaw, who was herself French, and white. She welcomed us and immediately told us we would not be able to use English after she finished telling us a story.

At the end, she asked, "What story did I just tell?"

I said, "You've told the story of 'Little Red Riding Hood.'"

She was shocked, and so were other class members, who thought I was putting them on. She asked me, "How did you know?"

I said I could tell from the way her voice went up and down, and up and down, by the cadences that the story *had* to be "Little Red Riding Hood."

From then on, she was sure I was going to be good in French—that I would be able to get work leading

French classes. I questioned that I would. But I knew being successful in her class was part of what I'd come there for. So I stayed in her French class the four years I was at Fisk, and I received a bachelor's degree in French in 1925. But I never taught it.

I made my way through other classes in a similar fashion. Even if I wasn't sure of the content, I found ways to be interested and to try to gauge what the professor was looking for. In philosophy class, for example, the teacher, who was the president of the university, assigned us Plato's allegory of the cave, about how we perceive what's real. I didn't understand the meaning of the allegory; but I didn't say I didn't know. I just tried to guess what the teacher wanted, as I had with the story of "Little Red Riding Hood" in French class.

Other teachers thought, "Oh, she must be smart."

The English teacher said to me, "You can do well if you take English." So I took English for four years. But by that time, I had come to understand what the allegory in the cave was all about. I wasn't brilliant, but I did better than the average students in some of my classes.

I thought about teaching, since it was one of the few professions open to women, along with social work. But I knew it wasn't likely I'd be hired by a white school system to teach a class in French. So I took courses in sociology as a backup. In my senior year, I lived and worked in the Bethlehem Center, a settlement house in Nashville, and decided to pursue social work as a career. When I went to Fisk, I walked back and forth two miles from the center to classes. At the settlement, I made my way teaching children and doing community organizing. When you're training, you're learning; you're trying out, finding out what's wrong and what's right.

At Fisk, you could go home at Christmastime, you could visit other people (provided your parents agreed), or you could stay at the school, where they had special holiday activities. Since I lived off campus, sometimes I stayed in a friend's dorm room at holidays.

On Christmas Eve, some of us went out and watched the moon. We looked for the star of Bethlehem. As we lay in the pitch-dark on the stone bench outside Jubilee Hall, we saw that star, and thought about the birth of the baby Jesus. That's when I truly knew what Christmas was about.

At breakfast on Christmas morning we came in all dressed up, the women in white and the men in black. The dining room was dark, except for candles, and some of us went through the room singing Christmas carols.

Everyone at the school for the holiday participated in the carols we all knew. We heard the Christmas story and we sang "Go Tell It on the Mountain, That Jesus Christ Is Born."

In 1924, my senior year, the art teacher asked us all to pick three paintings to copy; one was of a vase of sweet peas. I chose *The Good Samaritan,* and have cherished it ever since. My entire life has been driven by my emotional and spiritual response to the picture, and the message of compassion it communicates. My copy now hangs in the home of my second son, Paul, in Atlanta, Georgia.

I graduated from Fisk six months late because I stayed out of school for a semester in response to a boycott orchestrated by W. E. B. Du Bois, who wrote *The Souls of Black Folk*, published in 1903. He'd graduated from Fisk in 1888. By the time he arrived, the school offered courses in Latin, Greek, French, German, music, history, and moral theology. It had come a long way from its beginnings. After Du Bois left Fisk he began to agitate for the rights of his people, whatever they wanted to call us— Negro, colored, black. Now it's African American.

I don't follow just because someone else decides to lead. Hence, I wouldn't answer to what other people called me unless I'd been in on the decision-making process in the first place. No matter what you call us, we're the same people; we just press ahead through one thing or another.

Because of Du Bois's activities, some of the administrators didn't want him to come back to speak and maybe cause trouble. But when his daughter Yolanda was graduating in 1924, the Alumni Association chose him as their Alumni Speaker. So the administration couldn't say no. He came prepared to attack when he arrived to speak at commencement on June 2, 1924. His daughter had told him things, as had others, about what the administrator was doing that Du Bois considered belittling to the students. At times I thought so, too; he and I were concerned with the same things. He was the fighter, though.

At that time, Du Bois and Booker T. Washington were debating what to do about segregation and the plight of African Americans. Washington had been born in slavery and freed by the Civil War. He wanted us to start from where we were, to accept "separate but equal"—which wasn't equal at all—for the time being, and earn the respect of whites through hard work and education and economic gain. In terms of schooling, he stressed vocational training. But Du Bois, who was from Massachusetts and only experienced Jim Crow when he came south to Fisk, wanted to go beyond. He encouraged us to get a real education, not just training: "It is today that we fit ourselves for the usefulness of tomorrow." He wanted us to go deeper, to do and be more within ourselves, and in our school and church and country.

In *The Souls of Black Folk*, Du Bois claimed that Booker T. Washington's ideas would only perpetuate the conditions black people lived with. He pushed harder for personal advancement. At a time when whites wanted black colleges to teach students to accommodate to the Jim Crow laws, Du Bois was pushing back, especially on behalf of the "Talented Tenth," a phrase originated by northern white liberals, mostly Baptist missionaries, who supported the establishment of black colleges to train Negro elites. Du Bois was using it to describe the likelihood of one in ten black men becoming leaders of their race. With Jim Crow laws only put to rest by the Civil Rights Act of 1964 and the Voting Rights Act of 1965, the arguments of Washington and Du Bois were heard again as Malcolm X and Dr. Martin Luther King pursued very different civil rights agendas.

For his speech at the Fisk commencement on June 2, 1924, Du Bois used a title in Latin that meant "Silence Forevermore." But once he stood up and began to talk, there would be no silence forevermore—the opposite, in fact. He criticized the Fisk administration for being too preoccupied with money. In order to appease donors, the school forbade sororities; a student newspaper; fur coats and silk hose for women students; and touching between genders. If you walked on the sidewalk, the man or woman had to walk in front, so we couldn't touch.

Students had to wear uniforms off campus. Usually navy blue, they were made of cheap, washable fabric. The women wore long skirts and jackets and crisp white blouses. The idea was not to look well-off or showy, and on the other hand, to avoid an appearance that would broadcast "need."

In truth I didn't object to the uniform given that I had only one or two dresses to choose from when we had to get dressed for a supper or whatever. I didn't spend much time selecting. It was either this one or that one. But I didn't want to *have* to wear a uniform. That's where it became a problem—that we didn't have a choice in the matter.

All this was a way to regiment and keep control. The

president of the school not only wanted control; he felt he had to keep everything in line in order to satisfy the southern whites who contributed money. If you didn't follow the rules, you could be sent home, and perhaps not allowed back. The president made the decisions. There was a kind of disciplinarian in chief on campus who spied on the students and reported infractions. Some of us wanted a Negro, or black, or African American president at Fisk; the school didn't get one until 1947. Real change does not happen overnight. We wanted more freedom of choice in what we wore, where we went, whom we went with—all the things Du Bois was fighting for. He convinced members of his staff and the faculty to do things we hadn't done before. Du Bois added fuel to fires of protest that were already burning on campus.

In his speech, Du Bois directly attacked President Fayette McKenzie's administration: "I have never known an institution whose alumni are more bitter and disgusted with the present situation in this university. In Fisk today, discipline is choking freedom, threats are replacing inspiration, iron clad rules, suspicion, tale bearing are almost universal."

Immediately after Du Bois's speech, another young woman and I were supposed to perform a duet. The duet was sung by one person. I didn't remember a word of the song. I had totally forgotten it. Till today, I haven't remembered. I can account for it by saying that the whole occasion was traumatic; what Du Bois did was so disturbing. During the speech, and after it, some students were distressed, and voiced it, yelling, "Get rid of him," and all that.

I guess I was in shock. So were others. At Fisk, there were white women faculty members, several from Oberlin—which had the reputation of accepting blacks, as did the Quakers—who worked at the school for little if any salary. One of them, Miss Glass, the organist who played at meetings and had been sitting in front during Du Bois's speech, got up and ran up an incline out the door. She covered her ears so she couldn't hear what Du Bois was saying.

Not everyone disagreed with him; there were young people who picked up and went with him, and had meetings, and did everything the way Du Bois wanted—because I think they wanted it, too. After his speech, we had a student strike that went on for almost a year. I did not go on strike properly, because I didn't live in a dorm. I simply didn't go to classes for the first part of my senior year. During the strike, I stayed put at the settlement house. Others went home; some went to Howard University or other schools.

I didn't yell. I wasn't openly rebellious. I didn't fight, though many of the men did. The boys at Fisk grouped together and followed Du Bois's teachings. Though the girls didn't go around yelling and threatening, we were thinking the same thoughts as the boys; we, too, wanted the school to be more responsive to our needs and our rights. Du Bois was also able to persuade some faculty members about the needed changes. These were nice people—young and willing professors or teachers, some of them from Oberlin, like the organist who walked out on the speech. They were Quakers helping the needy, getting very little pay, if any; they were also sold on what was needed at the school. At first, President McKenzie paid no attention; then he pretended to pay attention.

Immediately after Du Bois's speech, some of the girls went around singing, and then sat down with the president. This didn't just happen one or two times; the commotion continued well after Du Bois left the campus. The guys in the Livingston dorm were under the watch of a matron, who was afraid of trouble. Some of them did start saying and doing dumb things. There was a lot of tension on campus then—and many more meetings. All through that summer, Du Bois spoke to people all over the country interested in what was happening at Fisk.

In the fall, several months after the commencement speech, male students overturned seats and broke windows in Memorial Chapel after promised reforms failed to materialize. At first, McKenzie had agreed to make some concessions after Du Bois's speech, as recommended by the school's trustees, but then he backed down. When a group of trustees arrived on campus in November 1924, they were greeted with cries of "Down with the tyrant!"

When the students rose up, chanting, "Before I'll be a slave, I'll be buried in my grave," the president called the police, who showed up in big numbers to smash up the men's dorms and arrest students, who could have been charged with felonies and put in prison. After they were finally released, the students called the strike, which went on for eight months, forcing the resignation of Fayette McKenzie on April 16, 1925. Eventually we were able to get things accomplished. Du Bois really stirred things up; but I was satisfied, and so were a lot of others in the end, when the dress code disappeared, elected student government came back, rules governing social life were brought up-to-date, and many of those who'd been expelled were let back into the school.

At Fisk, we had quarters. I went back for an additional quarter of classes until graduation in August 1925. Some of the students who didn't make it back after the strike still became part of the class of 1925; they were grandfathered in, so to speak. There were only eight of us who were graduated that summer. Our speaker was a professor, a medical doctor; they didn't have enough students graduating to qualify us for a grand send-off. Dr. C. V. Roman told the graduates: "You might think this is an ending—that you are fully educated now. It's called a commencement. It's not a beginning, but a continuing. You don't know everything when you graduate, but you need to know where to get what you ought to know."

Where would I get what I needed to know? After all, I had to support myself. I decided I was going to be a social worker. It seemed a natural progression after my work at the settlement house while still in school. At Fisk, we weren't just trying to get by; we were trying to learn how to be good citizens.

In 1925, after graduation, I went to work at a Congregational church in Raleigh, North Carolina, where I was satisfied, and would have stayed. I was financed by the American Missionary Association, part of the Congregational Church. For a salary of a hundred dollars a month, which was a goodly amount for those times, I directed the church's programs and activities. As part of my assignment, I had to raise as much money as I got; it was kind of a matching-funds concept. The AMA sent the church the money for my salary, and they in turn paid me. Many agencies and churches wanted to see that their money was well used and indeed got to the church that supported the various programs. The church in Raleigh was well satisfied with what I did.

I worked with children in the nursery school, and with the choir. I organized a group who put on a play. I developed programs for elderly people. I also had to do stenographic work for the pastor. In addition to all that, the pastor's wife often called me and expected me to do anything he was not available to do. Once there was a funeral, and Rev. DeBerry, the pastor, was late coming back from wherever he'd gone. The family of the deceased was ready to enter the church for the service, but the preacher wasn't there. So Mrs. DeBerry said, "Miss Smith, you have to lead the family in."

I was twenty-one. I didn't know anything about leading a funeral. I guess I got the hymnal, and started reading Scripture, and led them in. Shortly thereafter the pastor showed up to handle the rest of it. I did what I had to; in those days, we improvised and did the best we could with what was at hand. Once when I got sick, I was attended by a physician who turned out to be a brother of the now-famous Delany sisters, whose family lived in Raleigh, though they did not attend the church where I worked.

A friend from Fisk named Eliza Redd—that's two d's—who'd gone on to Cleveland, advised me to apply to Western Reserve University's School of Applied Social Sciences. Much later in 1967 it became Case Western Reserve University (CWRU) after merging with Case Institute of Technology. She sent me a letter saying, "There's an opening. If you apply, I am sure you will be able to enter. You'll have to find your own accommodations."

Western Reserve said they had a place for me, and they helped me get through with scholarships and work-study programs, as Fisk had. I was making my way. Over the years, my Fisk classmates and I tried to stay in touch; it wasn't easy, as we all scrambled to stay afloat. But two friends from Fisk, Myrtle Wiggins and Nell Baker Gwinn, were there to greet my firstborn son—honest, kind, and loyal they were, over all the years.

My friend and best classmate at Fisk in 1925 was a Catholic girl named Vera Baranco. We stayed in touch after we graduated; I visited Vera often. We were so close that I said to her, "I want you to be the godmother of my first child." But it didn't work out that way. Life took its turns.

The Barancos were from Louisiana and were mixed race. One of Vera's brothers was a medical doctor and another got a degree in dentistry from Meharry Medical School in Nashville. He would come to see his sister—and me. Some in the family thought I might become Catholic. When there was a holiday, I was invited along. During the Lenten season, we couldn't eat certain things. They didn't, and I didn't, either. One Easter, Mrs. Baranco sent a big box of food that looked delicious; but we couldn't eat it until after midnight. Those were the Lenten rules. And we couldn't have the light on in Vera's dorm room, because President McKenzie had instituted a 10:00 p.m. curfew at Fisk. So with the light that came through the transom, we returned to her room around 11:00 p.m. As far as we were concerned, the school didn't need to turn the light off on us. You did what you had to.

CHAPTER THREE

COMPASSION IN ACTION

And though I have the gift of prophecy,
and understand all mysteries, and all knowledge;
and though I have all faith, so that I could remove
mountains, and have not charity, I am nothing.

—1 CORINTHIANS 13:2

I graduated from what is now called Case Western Reserve University in 1928 with a master's degree in social sciences and practical training as a social worker. The agency where I worked was called Associated Charities. Later a new federal program was established to help support needy families and especially youth, encouraging them to do things to help chart their path after graduation. At the time, I didn't think it was exceptional for a woman to pursue a master's degree: what was special was the limitation on minorities. The school only accepted two a year on a racial basis. I am now the oldest living African American graduate of CWRU. I'm also one of the pioneers of the Fisk to Case Western Reserve Legacy Project.

The school's course work was good training for fieldwork, preparing students for issues we'd encounter with clients, such as finances, unemployment, domestic problems, and child rearing.

Though I never encountered outright bigotry at Western Reserve University, a lot of businesses and institutions had ways of letting you know you were not welcome. Nor was I able to strike up close relationships with faculty or other students due to lack of contact outside the classroom. Because the university didn't provide housing for graduate students, I rented a room, first on East Eighty-sixth Street, near Cedar, and then in the home of Althea Cavanaugh and her mother, Mrs. Ella Robinson, as well as her toddler son Bert, who remarked that I was always singing. Each of the tenants had a single room, as did Bert. He called my favorite song "Boo Kies," as in "Blue Skies." Bert was probably three years old when I moved into the home. He was a very alert little boy.

Once when he and his mother were talking about something, I joined in, taking Althea's side. Bert protested, pronouncing my name "Ahlmay."

"Ahlmay," he proclaimed, "you're not *in* this combersation." It wasn't my business! Although he did develop affection for me.

Mrs. Robinson and Althea and Bert became my Cleveland family, and remained so for years. I had little contact with Mama's family back in Dallas. But when I got word of my grandmother's death, I was able to go to the funeral because she left a small insurance policy, payable to me. I don't remember how much it was, but there was enough for me to pay the funeral expenses and get from Cleveland to Dallas.

To "make do," Mrs. Robinson and her daughter took in other boarders, too. I met them at Mt. Zion Congregational Church, United Church of Christ, where I worshiped, and where I am still a member to this day. I've been a member there for eighty-three years. I was referred to the church initially by Rev. DeBerry in North Carolina.

In my career as a social worker, I was always concerned with children in particular. At first, I was a worker for a family agency initially supported by private donations. When the federal government got involved, the program became Aid to Dependent Children—and the caseload increased. But when I first started it was called Mothers' Pension, a program set up in 1913 by the Ohio state legislature. Political progressives were concerned about the potentially negative effects of industrialization, immigration, and urbanization on children with single mothers left to raise them after their husbands died or abandoned the family. To prevent women from having to work outside the home while their children were young, a mother's pension was created with the funds from the county treasuries. Mothers originally received fifteen dollars a month for the first child and seven dollars a month for each additional child. Once a child reached the legal age for employment at fourteen, the payment stopped.

I went from one section of the program to an entirely new one, but was still helping the needy. Aid to Families with Dependent Children (AFDC), a federal assistance program in effect from 1935 to 1997, was administered by the United States Department of Health and Human Services. Aid to Dependent Children (ADC), created as part of the New Deal, was altered in 1960 with the addition of the words "families with," partly due to concern that the program's rules discouraged marriage.

When I worked for ADC in the mid-1940s, I helped place some children in foster homes and put others up for adoption, which was much more difficult and required a lot of preparation. Later I'd visit the foster homes to see how the youngster was adjusting. The job was very stressful because I could see how much people were suffering. Some people needed only financial help; others needed advice on making wise decisions about spending their money. As part of my program, I helped them find places to get things cheaper. I remember I told a woman once, "Go to the A&P; there's a special on such-and-such day, and you'll save because of the sale." Unfortunately, she went and bought so much that she couldn't take it home by herself. She had to hire a cab, and the cab cost more than she saved.

Then there were the Busters, a family I worked with in the 1940s. Mrs. Buster worked but didn't make enough money to support her three daughters, all of whom had different fathers. She decided to rent out the first and second floors of her house and moved her family into the basement. To me, that was her wanting to be as independent as she could be.

One of her daughters, Christine, who was smart and outgoing, told me at age nine that when she grew up, she wanted to be a judge. She didn't say "a lawyer"—no, it would be a judge for her. At that age, she had of course never been exposed to judges or lawyers. But as time passed, she was discovered to be a wonderful dancer.

Mrs. Buster was the sort of person determined to be

as ambitious as she could be, and to work at it. When she went to school, most people would introduce her as Christine's mother. She was one of my first studies. She was ahead of her time in watching the food she gave her children: there was no beef, no pork, no real butter allowed in the house, but margarine. Mrs. Buster was an early advocate of so-called health food. The children, of course, ate what she put on the table in front of them.

Over the years, I worked with the family and kept in touch with Christine's teachers, to ask how she was coming along. When she graduated, I went to my sorority, Alpha Kappa Alpha (AKA), and said, "Here is a child who wants to go to college."

AKA was founded at Howard University in Washington, D.C., in 1909. There are over a thousand chapters across the country now. The Great Lakes region alone has forty-six graduate chapters and thirty-nine active undergraduate chapters. AKA aims for a legacy of "sisterhood and service," since it was started by an educated group of African American women who knew how privileged they were, one generation away from slavery. The group was always active supporting community and government programs. I joined when I moved to Cleveland in the same year I became a member of the Mount Zion

Congregational Church. It was especially meaningful to me, given that at Fisk, sororities had been banned.

At AKA meetings we prayed, we sang, we did things not only to help ourselves but also to help people elsewhere. I was glad to participate in the sorority's programs but never liked the initiation rituals, which are kept highly confidential. It seemed that we should be able to welcome a newcomer without embarrassing her. If I'd signed up at a time when these rituals were required, I would have walked out.

But there is no denying the good work AKA did, and continues to do. AKA activities included not just socializing, but also supporting jobs programs, specifically the Cleveland Job Corps Center. We were supplementing what the federal government gave. It was these programs I was thinking of when I applied to help Christine Buster. According to relief regulations, any extra money Christine earned had to go toward the family's expenses. But I was able to prove that there were other people interested in helping her; so she was allowed to keep some of her earnings for school.

I also approached the House of Wills, a funeral home that had a program for helping people. Cheryle Wills was in charge of distributing funds to the needy.

The family gave Christine Buster financial help as well as work for the summer anytime she was in Cleveland.

In her early years at Ohio State, Christine's advisor called me and kept in touch about her progress. The advisor notified me that Christine was not only a good dancer but also had the makings of a choreographer. When she graduated, I attended because her family had no money to do so. She did very well and was highly respected. After Christine graduated, she got involved with the Karamu Theater, part of the artistic programs at a local settlement house near where her family lived, and taught in the Cleveland public schools.

When I worked for Aid to Dependent Children, one of my other clients was a widow named Louise Stokes, then struggling to raise two boys. I had particular empathy for her because her situation mirrored mine. I helped the family secure financial aid until Louise found work. Mrs. Stokes had been making more money as a domestic worker than she got from ADC. But she wanted to take care of her children. She was a scrupulously honest woman. The Stokes children were smart kids who did their homework. One of her sons, Louis, became a fifteen-term U.S. congressman representing Ohio's Twenty-first District, later the Eleventh, after redistricting; Carl became mayor of Cleveland, the first African American mayor of a major U.S. city.

Retired congressman Louis Stokes remembers: "My mother made eight dollars a day plus carfare as a domestic worker. The carfare was a significant element because we had streetcars then and sometimes she had to change two or three times to get to a single job. Her work varied: Sometimes she'd stay on a job all week. Other times she went back and forth to accommodate the needs of several families in a week's time. Around 1937, when I was a twelve-year-old boy, she was on the federal program then called Aid to Families with Dependent Children. Our allotment was thirty-five dollars a month.

"I recall two of our social workers, Mrs. Hedges and Mrs. Johnson, who was then Mrs. Cheeks. Both of them were our social workers when we resided at 2234 East Sixty-ninth Street, in the central area of Cleveland. Later we moved to the Woodland area, where we lived in a public housing project known as the Outhwaite Homes. I do not recall us being on welfare when we moved there. Both Mrs. Hedges and Mrs. Cheeks stood out to my brother Carl and me because they came to our home. If they arrived and discovered that our mother wasn't home at the time, they would not try to interact with us. In that era, social work had a different approach. The workers had to look around the home to see if there were signs of a male in the house, or of any recent acquisitions that indicated money was coming in. It was almost like police work. My impression of Mrs. Cheeks was that she was doing a tough job with compassion. She wanted to help us more, but was restrained by provisions of the law. I recall her as being a very nice lady."

Now eighty-four years old, Louis Stokes caps a career that included being a trial lawyer and a U.S. congressman for thirty years, with a role as Distinguished Visiting Professor at Case Western Reserve's Mandel School of Applied Social Sciences. At the request of professors, he goes into classes to lecture on such topics as welfare reform, public policy, civil rights, and the legislative process. The MA and PhD students at the school are all working as social workers while continuing their education. He finds it "incredibly rewarding to interact with students committed to helping build a more just society, working to eradicate the effects of injustice and discrimination."

It took me a while to catch up with the Stokes brothers, since they knew me as Mrs. Cheeks, not Johnson. On the occasion of my 105th birthday, which he attended, I received a lovely letter from Congressman Louis Stokes saying that I reminded him of the song "Ain't No Stopping Us Now"!

After taking early retirement in 1961, I'd frequently run into people who remembered me as their caseworker, and thanked me—even if I didn't always remember specifics about them. Once I ran into a woman on the bus who approached me as I got off, asking me if I was Mrs. Cheeks. Since I'd known her as a little girl, I didn't recognize this young woman. But when I asked where she'd lived, I recalled her situation.

Looking back, I'm satisfied that the career I chose, more or less accidentally, proved to be the right one: I've never regretted it. In many cases, I was able to help people improve their situations in life. Last year I received a letter from a former client named Ivan Foster, who informed me of his oldest daughter's graduation from Kenyon College, and his other daughter's National Merit Scholarship to Washington University in St. Louis. It's very gratifying to hear, "Thank God you played an important part in my early life." Now he passes on the wisdom he's gained.

I believe I chose my career wisely because in settings not formally designated as relevant to social work, I was able throughout my adult life to act on my interest in helping others financially and otherwise. After I retired, I began to travel; and in more than thirty countries, I saw things that motivated me to promote relief not just in this country, but also internationally.

CHAPTER FOUR

MY FIRST LOVE, MR. CHEEKS

Who can find a virtuous woman?
For her price is far above rubies.

—PROVERBS 31:10

Elmer Cheeks was a friend of Eliza Redd, the one who persuaded me to come to Western Reserve. She was a vibrant woman who later went off on a trip to Detroit and came back engaged to a southerner she'd met there. Eliza was a bit of what you'd now call a social butterfly. She had a male friend with whom she went to shows or played cards. So when this boyfriend of hers decided he was going to a party, he asked if Elmer could come with him. That's how I met Elmer—on a "double date" with Eliza, my fellow graduate student, and Walter. We all went to parties together.

Elmer and Walter fancied themselves men about town. Once they went to Montreal and stayed in a nice hotel. Walter had told Elmer that no matter where they went, he was going to publicly dunk his cookies in a big glass of milk. When they got to the hotel in Montreal, Elmer said, "I dare you . . ."

He didn't! Well, this was a special hotel. They thought they were living the high life.

Elmer had Native Americans and white people in his ancestry and could pass for white. We're all mixed; some just don't like to talk about it. I am not overcome with the idea "I'm white" or "I'm Negro," whatever. We have so many different names. I think that's because for so long this group was mistreated, and many of us pretended to be someone else. I know I did sometimes when it didn't seem I had a choice.

Elmer Cheeks wasn't only dashing; I'd also call him influential. Widely known and liked in the community in Cleveland, he was a professional with a good job—not to mention that at a tall and slender five feet eleven inches, Elmer was a real catch. He was congenial; he did things to please other people, including his family. He'd been raised in Virginia, the third of eight children, by a widowed mother. His father had been a carpenter and his mother a homemaker. His older brother Roy Cheeks came to Cleveland for work and became a lawyer specifically to learn how to get around the laws that kept us back. Elmer's sister Lena worked at the U.S. Mint in

Washington. It was a family in which the children grew up expecting to achieve something. The two oldest set a pattern for Elmer; he attended Purdue and graduated with a degree in electrical engineering.

He was much sought after. He was entertaining. If someone wanted a player to fill in at a bridge game, all he or she—usually she—had to do was call Elmer, and he came right away. They didn't need to plead. He liked bridge. In fact, before we got married, in order to be near him, I had to be ready to go to a bridge game no matter what else came up. I knew nothing about bridge, but I learned—never very well. Sometimes I would sit and listen, just to be there. And his friends accepted me.

Although he was sixteen years older than I was when we met in 1927, Elmer wasn't married. When we first met, I was twenty-three, and he was thirty-nine. I remember when he asked me how old I was, and I told him, he said, "Oh, no. That won't do. You're younger than Babe." Babe was his youngest sister. But we went ahead anyway, and it became the real thing. Before very long we were together. After a yearlong courtship, our engagement was announced at the Cavanaugh home. When I went to Baton Rouge to visit my college friend Vera Baranco and her family, Elmer telephoned every day. Some of those times, the homes I visited didn't even have a phone. I waited until I got home and then I asked him, "Why did you call as much as you did?" He said, "I just wanted them to know there was somebody who had a claim on you."

When it came time to consider getting married, I told Elmer I had decided when I was a student at Fisk that I would come back to marry in Memorial Chapel there. So in 1929 we went to Fisk to be married. On the way down we had to have a chaperone, because going from Cleveland to Nashville, we were going to be together overnight. Josephine Berryman, the other boarder in Mrs. Robinson's house, came along with us at our invitation. She was an excellent cook, and a person of strong character. Once at one of her parties, a guest asked about a dish she had served: "Oh, I like that; give me the recipe."

Josephine said, "Ma'am, if I gave you my recipe, you wouldn't have to pay me." She was nobody's fool. She worked hard and no doubt earned more than I did as a social worker. She had no education but she made good money and she made good food. Sometimes she'd come home late from a job and she'd wake me up at 11:30 or midnight to "come and have some of this good cake."

One day I said, "Please don't wake me up. I'd rather sleep than eat."

So Josephine went with Elmer and me to Nashville. I rode up front with Elmer, and she sat in the back.

I don't remember much about my wedding dress; but I know it didn't cost much. If I had anything special, it might have been provided by Josephine or by Mrs. Robinson. Elmer gave me both an engagement and a wedding ring. In my marriage vows I did not follow the traditional "love, honor, and obey," but instead said, "love, honor, and cherish." We didn't have the word *feminist* then; this is just what I saw as fair. I didn't discuss it with Elmer, nor did I do so years later with my second husband, Raymond Johnson. My intention was to say something different from what other people were saying. I would not agree to "obey." I was a grown woman, not a child. I didn't need someone whom I had to obey! But I could love, and do everything else other wives did.

There were about twenty people in attendance at the wedding at Fisk on September 23, 1929, including Ellen White, "my other mother" during my years at the school, where she worked in the administration. I met Mrs. White shortly after I arrived at Fisk, when I went to her office to ask a question. After that, she wound up taking me under her wing. I'd appreciated her kindness throughout my undergraduate days. When I was to be married, Mrs. White made the arrangements for the wedding itself and also encouraged other students to come. One of her three sons, Charles, was a Fisk graduate who worked for the legal department of the city of Cleveland. When she'd visit him, we'd get together. Her husband was the principal of one of the elementary schools in Nashville. One day I went with him to school during the strike at Fisk; because I had an education, I was a likely candidate to be a teacher. But once I saw the way his students behaved, I decided teaching wasn't for me. It was a turning point in my decision to be a social worker.

The new president of Fisk, Thomas Elsa Jones, a Quaker, a religious, honest, and kind man, and his wife provided our reception. They felt I deserved it if I'd come back to Fisk for my wedding. As I recall, the refreshments were cake and punch and nuts. Another man Elmer knew, Charles Spurgeon Johnson, and his wife invited us to be guests in their home for our wedding night. It was a wonderful experience. Elmer had also stayed with them the night before the wedding, while I stayed with Mrs. White. Elmer's friend Mr. Johnson became more and more important. There had been race trouble in Chicago, and he became part of the group trained to work on reconciliation—and he succeeded. He helped conceive the modern science of sociology and eventually became first African American president of Fisk in 1947.

Josephine rented a room and stayed until after the reception. Then she took a train or a bus back to Cleveland. Elmer and I started north by way of Knoxville, Tennessee. In 1929, there weren't as many people or cars on the streets as there are now. En route, Elmer read me a poem by John Greenleaf Whittier, an antislavery activist and a Quaker, about a Maryland woman who was about to be attacked because she hung the Union flag from her window as General Lee rode by. It quoted her as saying, "Shoot, if you must, this old gray head, but spare your country's flag."

The weather had been bad, and we were running into night. Of course, there were no lights. We just drove. When we reached an inn, Elmer took our luggage in and registered us. Then he came back for me. In the foyer, the manager said, "Your wife is a nigger."

Elmer was not one to swear. He said, "Who in hell called my wife a nigger?"

The man said, "Excuse me, excuse me, Miss," and we went to bed. When it was daylight, we didn't stay and have breakfast there, because Elmer was afraid of what might happen. So we drove on to Cleveland. On the way, he pointed out a sign that said, The South Won. These were actual road signs. If a southerner was talking about the North, as Elmer described it, he or she might say not the North won but that "We were defeated." The way the Confederate generals might have put it was, "We withdrew."

That's when I got interested in history, on my honeymoon, which consisted of our journey back to Cleveland. We didn't stop again after the stay in Knoxville until we got to Gettysburg; Elmer was a keen student of American history. We read the signs along there, too. I think I've been to Gettysburg once more since then. It's important to learn from history, about why people are the way they are.

As a newlywed couple, we set up house on Mount Overlook in Cleveland, where Elmer had purchased a home in 1914. Elmer loved not only the family we made in due course but also the family of which he had been a part. After he brought his mother and five younger siblings to Cleveland, he put them up in the house on Mount

Overlook. He was aiding his family's transition to the North. He and his brother Roy and sister Lena supported the household as different members of the family moved in and out, with their mother keeping house. At the time, the area was quite undeveloped, with very few houses. His brothers and sisters went to school supposedly in the district where the neighbors lived; but there came a time when the school system separated the races.

By 1929, when Elmer was going to be married, he might have felt uncomfortable telling his mother she was about to be displaced. But she did learn of the wedding. As the date approached, Elmer's brothers and sister told their mother they'd get an apartment or a house where she could stay, too. By the time Elmer carried me across the threshold of the house, the rest of the family had gone. But even after they left, one brother kept the key to the house. It was obviously hard for members of the extended family to give up their connection to the only home they'd known in Cleveland.

One Saturday night there was a knock on the door: It was the brother who had a key. I suggested Elmer call the family members and gather up all the keys.

He said, "No, I won't do it that way." Instead, he

said, "Let's replace the key." Elmer never did tell his mother he'd changed the lock. I don't know that we talked about it. Elmer simply operated on the basis that this was his house, and I was his wife. He just decided to do something to take care of it.

Overall, my in-laws didn't fuss with me. You know, I wasn't a good cook. Josephine started teaching me, but I couldn't do much. Someone in the family asked Elmer, "Is Ella Mae a good cook?" And he said, "Yes, but if she lost the cookbook, we'd starve to death."

Elmer was considerate. Before Sweetest Day, a holiday in the Great Lakes region that falls on the third Saturday in October, he asked me, "What kind of candy shall I buy you?"

I said, "Peppermint."

And he said, "Oh my, I won't have to spend much money on you."

There was such a difference between the cost of peppermint and chocolate. I don't like chocolate. When we were courting, Elmer would sometimes call me late on a summer night to go out for ice cream. He always got chocolate; I preferred vanilla—still do. After we married, I told him I didn't buy things—and I didn't want him to, either—that I didn't want. When we chose things to buy, or places to go, or what to eat, we made the decisions together. They didn't seem like decisions. It was just about finding out what I wanted for dinner today, and where I wanted to go tomorrow. Of course, what he wanted, I wanted, too. I had to make concessions, as he had. Marriage is all about compromises.

During World War I, all men were required to sign up for what was then called Selective Service. You had to register with the government. As an electrical engineer, Elmer realized there should have been opportunities for him to be an officer, but because of his race, he was not given the same privilege as whites. The military was segregated then. Given his degree, Elmer appealed to Newton B. Baker, a Clevelander who was what they then called secretary of war, and found an ordnance—or supply—job that enabled him to serve as an officer rather than a combat soldier. I don't think he got any more money than a private would have, but he had the opportunity to serve his country a different way.

When he came back from the service, Elmer went to teach in Texas at Prairie View A & M, which was part of HBCU (Historic Black Colleges and Universities). After being there for about a year, he'd returned to Cleveland and got a job at Cleveland's Municipal Light Division.

One day after we were married, we were having trouble with the lights.

I said, "You prepared for this; why don't you fix that light? Otherwise we'll have to have someone come in."

He said, "I am not an electrician." He explained that there was a big difference between an engineer who oversaw whole systems and the man who comes to repair the lines or the connections. He added, "I don't do electrical work. I plan and see that it goes into effect as it should." The electrician didn't make as much money or get as much respect.

From then on, I never asked him much about his job.

Elmer liked the arts. He had season tickets for the opera, opting for the cheaper seats in order to see more productions of the Metropolitan Opera when it was in Cleveland for Opera Week. It was a big social event each spring. Elmer also called together friends who, like him, wanted to get everything out of the opera that they could. He'd invite them to the house to go over the content of the opera beforehand, so they'd know what to expect at the performance. Elmer took for granted that if he explained it to them, and actually played a record of something that was being performed, they would understand, as he did.

Once before we were married, when he was on duty—because he worked nights sometimes in city hall—even though he was working, he decided we would go to the opera anyhow. He stopped by our house and I got in the car. We went to city hall first, where he changed from his work clothes to those he would wear to an opera. Everyone dressed formally for the occasion, no matter where their seats were; and we wanted to look our best. Afterward Elmer changed again when he went back to city hall so there'd be no evidence of where he'd been.

In Cleveland, Elmer joined a church that still exists, St. John AME Church. The people at the church were proud of the success he had with a program there for boys. At a meeting of a combination of churches—you'd have different chapters and so on—Elmer was asked to describe what he did with the boys to make the program so successful. So he told them. One man got up and said, "You're teaching our boys, but you play cards on Sunday, and you go to the movies on Sunday."

After that, Elmer decided he didn't need church. He had no time for people who told him who was sinning, and who wasn't. Later when we were married, he did all he could to make me comfortable. He took me to various meetings, choir meetings, business meetings, and helped me support the church, even though he didn't attend services.

From my perspective, we had a very strong love affair. Elmer Cheeks was sound in his thinking and confident enough to tell the truth. He was faithful, loyal, generous, and ambitious. And he had a sense of humor. Once he related an incident and I said I didn't remember it that way. He replied, "Would you call me a liar for trying to make a good story better?" His quick wit made him so much fun; he seemed to find joy in everything we did together.

I developed an interest in the theater when Elmer got involved in a theatrical troupe called the Gilpin Players, named after the black actor Charles Gilpin, who traveled throughout the United States. Gilpin had started his career in minstrel shows and played his first dramatic roles in Chicago. He came to Cleveland to appear in Eugene O'Neill's *The Emperor Jones* at the Hanna Theatre on Fourteenth Street, between Euclid and Prospect, a role he'd originated on Broadway to great acclaim. Gilpin later lost the signature role in the London production to Paul Robeson after a falling out with O'Neill over the use of the word *nigger* in the play, and never regained his career momentum. Elmer and some of the others at Karamu House, where he was active, attended the Cleveland production and later invited Gilpin to come see them in their little theater. And he did. The Karamu Players were renamed the Gilpin Players in his honor.

The settlement house on East Thirty-eighth and Central had been established in 1915 by Russell and Rowena Woodham-Jelliffe, Oberlin graduates with something of the attitude of missionaries. They didn't pay themselves regular salaries. People both white and nonwhite contributed to programs at the house, which was what we'd now call a community center. There was a program for children, for married couples, for people who needed help in learning how to cook and housekeep—those sorts of things. And then there were people who came in and wanted to act. It was essentially a social service agency, but one with an artistic element.

In the 1920s after many African Americans came to Cleveland from the South, the Jelliffes resisted pressure from neighbors to exclude them from programs at the center, and soon found the settlement house a magnet for talented African American musicians and dancers and painters. Elmer committed himself to a number of programs there and grew very close to the Jelliffes. The immediate community was mostly black, and people there didn't have a lot of money to give to help support the center. But some were teachers and lawyers, and did contribute. You could become a member no matter who you were, as long as you had the interest.

Years later a well-known artist named Paul Travis, who worked in the Glenville area, decided to go to Africa. The Jelliffes and others asked him to bring African memorabilia and other things they could use in the house. It was only after he came back with various African artifacts that the word *Karamu,* a Swahili word that means "a place of joyful gathering," was used. The Playhouse Settlement became "Karamu" in 1941. Karamu is still an active force in the arts community in Cleveland and is listed in the National Register of Historic Places as the oldest African American theater in the country. Many of Langston Hughes's plays were developed and premiered there.

Even though Elmer didn't always appear in the dramas at Karamu, after we started dating I knew that if I was going to have any time with him, I had to be ready to go with him to the theater, even if just to socialize and support the Gilpin Players. When they were constructing or planning the theater, Elmer helped with that. It didn't matter to me or to him whether he was in the play. He was going to be there, and one of the things that I had to do if I wanted to be with him was be there, too. He liked drama, and music, all of it—and so did I. I remember when the Jelliffes were planning a twenty-fifth anniversary of the program. Elmer couldn't go, but Mrs. Jelliffe wrote a letter I kept for years, expressing her appreciation of him, and all that he'd done for the program. She said to him, "More than anyone else, Russell and I could depend on you."

She appreciated that Elmer didn't take things at face value. He was an engineer, after all, and had an inquiring mind. Mrs. Jelliffe said that in her view, Elmer wanted things to be done properly; and she highly valued that he didn't tell her and her husband what they wanted to hear, necessarily. There were other people at the program who were not as forthcoming, and they went along because they wanted to be friendly with the Jelliffes. Elmer may not have been one of the outstanding actors at Karamu House, but he was reliable, and sound in his thinking. He seemed confident that he could tell the Jelliffes what he really thought.

Elmer was forty-one when we married. He really wanted his first child to be a boy. He had looked forward to having a family, beginning with a son. He had talked about it so much. All these years, many men had families and sons; but Elmer didn't. He did have a lot of opportunities. After we got married and I was pregnant, he kept talking about his son. He predicted it was going to be a boy—*his* son. At that point, he didn't say "our son." I was agreeable. I wanted to have a child, too. I wanted to have his child. As soon as I could have a child legitimately, I did. James, whose full name is Elmer James Cheeks Jr., was born in 1930, and our second son, Paul, in 1936. Jim and Paul don't have to guess their ages, like I did. They can see a certificate. They can ask me or they can look at records. That's the way it is. Jim came twenty-four hours and ten minutes after he was expected. He was supposed to be born on the Fourth of July, but he was a day and an hour and ten minutes late, and ran into July 6. Althea Cavanaugh became godmother for my firstborn son, whose relationship with her son Bert was like that of a sibling.

Jim was born in the middle of the Depression. Although Elmer and I didn't have much in the bank, we lost it all after Black Tuesday, when the stock market crashed. We both kept working and trying to keep up. Everyone in the neighborhood was in the same situation. I went back to work when Jim was about six weeks old. The social agencies would hold your place open for five or six weeks, period. They didn't force you to leave; but it was understood that you would leave for so many weeks. Because they were not only careful about me; they wanted my offspring to be a concern as well. I worked, and Elmer helped with child rearing to the extent that he could, given physical limitations due to an illness. Sylvia, Elmer's sister, helped us once I returned to social work.

There's no comparison between what babysitters were paid then and what they get now. If I worked as a housekeeper today I would get much more than I did as a social worker; how much more, I don't know. As far as our earnings, Elmer took care of the regular expenses, and as I remember, we bought a car from my salary. I don't recall what those earnings were; but they were enough to enable me to chip in. Because of that, we were able to afford the car of our choice. Elmer and I were better off than many in that we were both professionals, with advanced degrees—unusual in those days.

After we knew Paul, our second child, was coming, Elmer decided that he was going to give me the girl I hadn't had. He had his son; I should have my girl. He would go around to his friends, who knew we were expecting a baby, and tell them, "It's going to be a girl." Instead of arriving on February 12, Paul came a few hours earlier. His birthday is February 11. Elmer welcomed Paul as he had Jim; of course, I did, too.

Jim was always serious-minded, self-sufficient, and studious. He had the manner of a child older than his years. Once when he was about three, he met my friends Myrtle Wiggins and Nell Baker Gwinn at the door to our home on two consecutive Sundays. On the second Sunday, he said, "What, *again*?" Either he or Paul called my dear friend Myrtle "Mugga Wiggums."

Once when Jim was a very little boy, age three or four, Elmer and I took him to church, where the pastor talked in his sermon about the way people get money. He declared that some people say, "Get money, get money, get money any way you can—but get money."

Then this very young voice piped up "Get money, get money . . ." and repeated it.

Reverend Brown said, "Well, I know there's one person here today who was listening."

Jim was devoted to Paul during their childhood. I remember Jim taking Paul to his room without comment when I seemed hard on his younger brother, and his lighting the tree on Christmas morning and dragging Paul down the stairs on his back until he realized that Paul's feet were dragging on the stairway. Thereafter on Christmas, Paul came downstairs under his own steam. Paul was affectionate, gregarious, and great at making and keeping friends.

Elmer was a loving and doting father who died of what they now call Lou Gehrig's disease, in 1941 at age fifty-three. He worked until the day before he died. We'd been married from 1929 to 1941. Now I was on my own at thirty-seven with two boys, who reacted in very different ways to their father's death. At the time, Jim was ten and Paul was five. Neither Paul nor Jim had the symptoms of Elmer's disease. When Paul was on the way, the doctor told me the disease was transmitted by the mother, not the father. So the boys were safe.

We all admired Elmer's patience and bravery during a long and difficult illness. The problem had first been noticed at a celebration of Jesse Owens's four gold medals in the 1936 Olympics. When the team returned from Berlin, Elmer and I attended a parade honoring Owens. On the way from the car to the park, one of our friends said to Elmer, "Why didn't you buy shoes big enough? You're limping a little."

We went to two or three doctors. One said his condition was muscular atrophy. But another said it was muscular dystrophy.

Elmer was in a wheelchair for many years prior to his death. He couldn't walk. He couldn't even hold his cards at bridge—I did it for him. I would shuffle them, place them, and then open up his cards so that he could see them. At the proper time, he would bid, and I would play when it was his turn. He would bid, but I had the cards—though I wasn't to say "bid."

After a while, it got to the point where Elmer couldn't chew his food and had to have strained vegetables, soups, and sauces. We had caretakers who bathed Elmer and took him to the toilet. Coworkers took him to work. He was determined; and although all these things seemed hard, he worked around them. He responded with grace to all his challenges.

Years later, my granddaughter, Audrey, came to live with me; her mother had serious health issues after childbirth. Because her mother was Catholic, my first grandchild was baptized in that church.

Now fifty years old, Audrey Wehba recalls: "When

my grandmother talked about Elmer, you could hear the love in her voice, even after fifty years or more. She talked about their dating, and about trust and sacrifice in marriage: how Elmer would watch the boys so she could go out now and then, because they would both enjoy and appreciate each other more when they were together. She also talked of Elmer's illness and death. One story has always been especially poignant for me. He was a tall man and she is quite petite. When his illness was advanced and he lost his motor control, Elmer would ask her to move out of the way if they were walking together if he knew he was going to fall, so he wouldn't hurt her by falling on her."

One day Elmer went to work and worked a half day before he had to come home. The person who was there taking care of the boys called the doctor, and said, "Mr. Cheeks is ill, and you ought to come and see him."

The housekeeper called me at work. When I approached the house, I was told the doctor was inside. He said to me, "Mrs. Cheeks, I'm afraid he won't last through the night."

I called Mrs. Ella Robinson, Althea Cavanaugh's mother. Over the years, the family had continued their interest in me. They did not provide for me financially, but they were like family. Mrs. Robinson was really the one in charge in the household. They always came when they thought they were needed. They helped whatever way they could. They said, "I care" or "I'm sorry." People like them have taken me where I am.

Mrs. Robinson came right away after I told her about Elmer's condition. She was with me when Elmer died, around 1:00 a.m. Before Elmer passed, she told him, "Ella Mae has been a good wife."

The man who lifted and carried and bathed Elmer was also in the room when my husband died. Mrs. Robinson was my companion through this ordeal—and thereafter. When it happened, I did not wake up Jim. It wasn't wise—or necessary. At that time, his room was in the attic. When Jim came downstairs to the second floor, I was back in bed, or at least in the bedroom. I told him, "Your father died last night."

I don't recall what he said, but I followed it up with, "You knew he was ill."

He replied, "Not *that* ill." I didn't say anything more. Jim knew what was going on. He'd actually been baptized earlier when Bishop Phillips came to the house to give Elmer the last rites when he got noticeably weaker.

Elmer truly loved me and the boys.

After his father died, Jim refused to talk to me about it. Later a child psychiatrist told me he'd done that to keep me from crying. He wanted to protect me. Given that Paul was only five at the time, I thought he might fear I'd leave him, too; so I never actually mentioned his father's death. The night it happened, I'd sent him away to a house on the same street, but with another family. From their home, Paul could see our front entrance.

"When someone opens the door, why do they hug Mama?" he asked.

Beezie, the friend who was watching Paul, didn't tell him why. Paul did not go to his father's funeral. Jim did.

One day Paul said to me, "Mother, when I grow up, I am not going to leave you. I am not going to go to Detroit. I am going to stay with you." Why Detroit? I never knew. Months later as we passed Lakeview Cemetery, I realized Paul still didn't understand what "death" meant, when he asked, "Does Daddy still limp?" When he was older, I took him to the grave site. We'd sit, but we wouldn't talk about his father. It was quiet, and we could be alone.

CHAPTER FIVE

CARRYING ON

Rise, Shine, for Thy Light Is a Coming

—TRADITIONAL SPIRITUAL

My husband Elmer never danced. I liked to dance. But after Elmer died, I had problems in social situations. People asked me to dance when I was available, but I could not accept a man's invitation because then his wife would be sitting by herself. Why would a wife be a wallflower while I was dancing with her husband? It would be hurtful. She's come to have fun with her husband, and he's off dancing with someone else.

So I didn't dance with the gentlemen in question: we visited, we talked. I would go to parties as a widow if I knew the hostess felt it was all right for me to attend. There were many things I could go to, even if I couldn't dance. But the hostess had to approve and not wonder if having too many single ladies roaming the room would cause difficulty for married couples.

When they were very young, my sons and I had to adjust to one another. We had to make a new life, the three of us. I hadn't been around many children at that point in my life. I had no example of what children should be allowed to do or not do. But I wanted so much that they would be what they could be, the best they could. By nature, I'm a worrywart. Raising children, I learned the true meaning of patience—of being careful, considerate, not feeling we had to do everything all at once, or to make this decision or that one right then and there. Trying to be both mother and father, I may have been too hard on my sons at times. But they are now loving and devoted fathers as well as successful professionals. So it all came right in the end. My family, I believe, respects me. I know they love me.

I was trying to be a father, or do a father's job. Paul likes sports. When Elmer was alive we had a radio, and Paul was exposed to broadcast baseball games. Soon after my husband died, the Cleveland Indians had what they call a "ladies' day" game at which women got a reduced rate. I took Paul and some of his friends. It was a doubleheader.

Paul told me, "Mother, I want to be at the park around eleven."

I said, "Honey, the game doesn't start until one."

He said, "But I want to get the players' autographs."

So we left home at about 10:00 a.m., and he got his autographs. Because it was a doubleheader, we didn't get home until around 9:00 p.m.

I said, "Paul, you can go to any game, any time, but I am not going to leave home at ten in the morning and get home at nine at night. You'll have to go by yourself."

Trying to be both mother and father, I had to plan everything. I thought, "Is this more expensive than that?" Jim and Paul did their best to help me. Since I didn't drive, we had no car after Elmer died. Jim and Paul and I would all go to the grocery store; they'd help me bring the packages home.

It wasn't easy being mother and father at the same time. Jim wanted a BB gun. The requests began after Elmer's death. I wasn't too keen on getting him one, but one of Elmer's friends said, "At this age, boys like to have BB guns."

Elmer's friend bought the gun and gave it to Jim. One day Jim took it out from the back room into the yard and pulled the trigger. I heard the sound it made, then Paul crying. When I went out, I saw that Jim had picked up a dirty rag from the ground and was trying to eliminate the blood. The pellet hit Paul just above the eye. Jim loved his brother. But he'd shot him by accident.

I took away the gun and said, "Let's go in," and then I said, "We won't keep the gun anymore."

There was nothing more about BB guns. Jim didn't argue. It wasn't important. He cared about his brother a great deal. Paul always wanted to do what his big brother did. That brotherly love remains. It's expressed in various ways now, as it was then.

After we'd moved from Mount Overlook to the Glenville area, we had to make arrangements for Paul to get home from school. By that time, Jim attended what they called junior high school. Normally he would have been at a school called Patrick Henry; but a friend named Genevieve Storey advised me that all I needed to do was apply at the Board of Education and give a good reason why Jim would not stay at Patrick Henry. My good reason was that Jim needed to go by Paul's school and bring him home every day.

Then one day Jim said, "Mama, I don't want to pick up Paul anymore. He's a showoff. He wants to get everyone's attention. It embarrasses me."

So I said, "Paul, don't embarrass Jim." My older son had his reasoning; he had the right to tell me. And Paul couldn't just do what he wanted. From then on, they got along well. Jim did his thing and Paul did his.

Once I started to hit Jim. That's the way many of us disciplined our children then. Jim said nothing. He just took my hand and moved it. He didn't pull it; he just grabbed it. He was about fourteen at the time.

I remember saying to myself, "He's fourteen, and six feet tall—what could I do if we had a fight?" But I had my methods.

I think there's a way to discipline without spanking. You don't have to hit your children. Sometimes you have to just put them in the corner. That's what we used to do, too—have them sit and think about what they've done. But that's for when they're young. Teenagers are a different story.

Paul remembers: "I must have been about thirteen or fourteen years old when I determined that I was larger and stronger than my mother. As I frequently did in those days, I did something my mother felt was inappropriate and she announced, in no uncertain terms, that I was grounded that following weekend. It was my assumption that she could not physically stop me, so I stated this, and added that I was going out anyway.

"Feeling very cocky that evening, I went to take a

shower to get ready to join my friends. When I completed my shower, I went to my room to dress. When I looked into my closet and checked my dresser, all of my clothes were gone! In answer to my shouts of frustration, my mother reminded me that she'd said I was not going out. She had made sure by hiding my clothes.

"This was one of the many times I realized that though my mother might be small in stature, she was a force to reckon with."

When Jim was sixteen, he was accepted into a special program. He'd done well on a radio show called *Quiz Kids,* and been noticed when he excelled in school. When the University of Chicago developed an accelerated program, Jim took the entrance tests and was accepted. One summer we'd taken a trip to Washington and visited the Howard campus; but Jim decided Chicago was the place for him.

I had received a questionnaire from the university that had to be signed by the principal of John Adams High School of the Cleveland School District, where Jim was a student. I had Jim take the questionnaire to the principal, but I didn't get it back. So I called and told him I was waiting. The principal responded that he hadn't sent it because he didn't approve of the fact that some schools were taking our brightest children.

I said, "But I didn't ask for your permission. I would like for you to send it."

He sent it. Instead of entering the eleventh grade at John Adams High School of the Cleveland School District, Jim skipped the eleventh and twelfth grades and entered the University of Chicago as a sophomore.

Jim liked music. He liked the opera. In this, he followed his father's example. Paul was his own person; he had ambitions, too. Like his engineer father, my younger son liked building things. He attended and graduated from Kent State University with a degree in architecture. The accomplishments of both my sons and their families have made me very proud.

The same year Jim was accepted into a special program at the University of Chicago, I cashed in an insurance policy that matured several years after Elmer's death. We had to decide as a family what to do with the money. With his share of the insurance, Paul decided on a bicycle. Jim decided on a trip to New York, where he wound up permanently years later. The two of us went. Once we got there, he went his way and I went mine—though he did talk me into going to the Statue of Liberty.

I looked up and up and up. He was determined to climb up into the crown. We were going to the top, to look over. I said, "Jim, I can't do that."

He said, "But Mother, that's the only reason I wanted to come to New York."

He'd lost his father six years before, but he was still my little Jim.

I thought, "I'm afraid there's going to be an accident. But if something happened to Jim, and I wasn't there, I'd feel guilty." So I went, scrambling to get up and down, up and down. When it was over, and I tried to move, I thought, "I can't; it hurts too much." When I got home, I could hardly walk. I couldn't even go to church.

Actually, I wasn't thinking, "Oh my God, I've got to be a good mother." I wanted to be a good mother, and I made decisions about things I felt my sons would enjoy according to what they expressed. I never felt that when I spent this or that, I was getting rid of something; I felt I was getting something. My sons were reaching, and they need to be helped.

Jim and I agreed that from New York, he would go on to the University of Chicago. Back in Cleveland, after a few hours I called the airport and said, "My son took a flight from New York to Chicago. Do you know if he got there safe?"

The man laughed and said, "Well, Madam, we haven't heard that there was any trouble with the plane."

When Jim went to Chicago, I felt I had no further control over him. One night when he came home, he went out to the theater and didn't get back home until 1:00 a.m. I was walking the floor.

He came in and I said, "Hi. I didn't know what you were doing or if you were safe."

Jim replied, "Mother, I lived in Chicago all these months and you didn't know what I was doing."

I said, "That's true."

I told myself not to tell him if I worried again. I didn't consider he was insulting me; but it brought me up sharp. He was considerate except where it interfered with his thinking. Then he wouldn't necessarily argue: he just wouldn't make any comment.

When he came back from the university once, he had his hair long. I said, "Jim, it embarrasses me. You don't want people to think I'm the kind of mother that just lets you get by with it."

But by that time, he was his own person. Once when

I was shopping for Jim, and had him with me, we saw a shirt that was better made than the others. After looking at the price, I totally ignored his choice and bought another shirt based on the cost. When he came back from Chicago, that shirt was with his clothing, the tag still on it. I didn't talk to him about it. But I told myself to let him do his own clothes shopping from there on in, or to wait and buy the better things when I had the money.

After he went off to Chicago, Jim didn't go to church much. Once he'd left the house, whether or not he did so was his business. Paul went, not to learn about Christ, but because he had friends who got together there and made plans to do things. I didn't worry about that!

Paul was always making friends and keeping them. He loved the idea of family and added unrelated people to our family whenever he could. His ideas about unchaperoned parties for teenagers were ahead of his time. I couldn't always keep up with what Paul was doing. I didn't think I should have to keep up with a young man when he's having fun—as long as it was nothing serious. Sometimes I wanted to tell him, "Honey, you mustn't say that." But then I just stopped and I thought, "I just hope you'll be the kind of man your father was." Elmer had had a good time as a young man. He enjoyed being with people.

Once when Paul accompanied a friend to a meeting at the YMCA, the man at the door told Paul that his friend, who was Italian, could come in, but he couldn't: "You should go to your own, down at Seventy-eighth and Cedar; that's the one for your people." But that YMCA was far away from where we lived. Paul went home like he was supposed to, and his friend went with him. I called Perry Jackson, a politician who at one time was on the Metropolitan YMCA board.

Perry said, "Send Paul back. When he goes back, he won't have any trouble."

But Paul said, "No, I won't." He was probably eleven or twelve at the time. He was concerned that his friend Chucky would be embarrassed.

The summer before Jim went back to Chicago, I didn't want him to spend his time lying around and reading the paper and listening to the radio. He'd gone to a summer camp in Springfield, Massachusetts, when he was about twelve. But now he was sixteen, past the allowed age of fourteen; so he could get a work permit. He was tall and very mature-acting, and I thought if he got a job in that neighborhood, the owner would have him do adult work, but he would be paid a fourteen-year-old's wages.

I called the staff at the settlement house, later known as Karamu, knowing they wouldn't have anything in the budget for him. So I told the director I wanted Jim to help with one of their programs, and I would give the settlement house fifteen dollars a week for his pay—but I wouldn't tell Jim about it. His job would be escorting small children to and from an elementary school.

When I told Jim about the job, I said, "You will get fifteen dollars a week, and you should save five dollars, spend five dollars, and contribute five dollars to household expenses."

He said, "Mother, five dollars isn't going to help pay the family's bills."

I said, "No, but at least you will be doing something."

I don't relish the idea of telling people what they should do. I don't think I rule the world. I don't accept that I am always right.

When I told my children to do so-and-so, I didn't say, "Because I'm your mother." I said, "We are a family. We've got just so much money." After all, my sons had to learn how to get along with other people, as well as with me.

As time passed and he got older, the opportunities for Jim changed. But the plan for dividing the money stayed the same. There came a time when Paul said to me, "Mom, I can't pay a third of my money to the house because I have a date, and she needs a corsage."

I said, "Let's think about that. Of course, she needs a corsage. Why don't we decide together that you will pay the house later? I can't say to the grocer, I can't say to the telephone man, I can't say to all the places where we pay bills that we can't pay. We can't just let all that go. But suppose we advance it."

All he could think about was the corsage—not paying the phone bill. Paul liked people, and wanted them to approve of him. Jim didn't care as much what other people thought.

Once when Paul was about fourteen he was given an assignment in class that was due at the end of the month. When I asked him about it, he'd say, "I've got time; I've got time"—day after day after day, until the night before it as due. That evening he told me he'd do it. But one of his friends called and asked him to do something or other.

He told me, "I'll do it in the morning." But he didn't wake up in time, and he didn't get a good grade.

He said to me, "That teacher is prejudiced; she's white, and she worked out some way to flunk me."

I said, "Yeah, I understand that. She stayed up all night, Paul, trying to find out what she needed to do to flunk you."

Now Paul is married to a white woman. Times have changed!

Paul liked to have a lot of things. As he grew up, I think he fashioned himself a bit of a dandy. He wanted to dress like Cab Calloway. I didn't care for the zoot suit look. Finally, he decided that the only way he could be sure that he was going to have what he wanted in clothes was to wear them out of the store.

He would buy them, and then if I said, "Take it back," he would say, "Mom, they won't take them back. I've worn them." We had different ways of handling each other.

One day we went shopping and he bought a black hat. Bishop Phillips was a bishop, and dressed like one, in the type of hat the bishops were wearing. So Paul went out one day and bought a hat like Bishop Phillips's with his own money.

When he wore it home, I said, "Paul, that looks like the hat Bishop Phillips wears." I don't recall his answer, but I don't doubt that it was snappy. He took his outfits seriously.

He had some shoes, pink ones. I said, "I don't like that color. Take it to the shoe repair shop and have them dyed black." So he did. I guess he tried to meet me halfway. Overall, my children pleased me. Whatever happened, right or wrong, I held my sons responsible for their behavior. I didn't say, "Oh, I was a bad mother," if things didn't go my way. I gave them the opportunity to think things through for themselves; but I also had backup plans, just in case.

In retrospect, I might have overdone it, trying to have boys my neighbors and friends would describe as "well trained—good boys who behave." They could have walked out and said, "To heck with you; I want to do this, and I'm going to do that." Overall, we handled things. Often we decided that things that came up and caused disagreements weren't worth a fight. It wasn't worth being angry with each other, because so many times when we are angry, we're not ourselves. We're not at our best.

I think that in many things I succeeded as a mother.

At least I hope I did. Both my sons are industrious. If I failed, so be it. It's too bad. But I can't undo it. I can't make it over, and at this point, I can't add to it or take from it. I look at my sons and I hear them speak to me and about me, and I guess I didn't fail.

Jim Cheeks remembers: "Raising two less-than-perfect sons during wartime, my mother taught us about grammar, consideration for others, music, and the public world. And one special thing: though she had suffered indignities and injustices in the South and even in a not-always-welcoming Cleveland, her lesson was education, work, independence, self-reliance, not victim-hood."

I don't know anyone who dislikes my sons. Jim is quieter, and he doesn't go out looking for friends. But I have never heard anyone say, "I don't like Jim."

I've heard any number of people, including Elmer's sister, call my younger son "my sweet Paul," as she held him.

One day Paul said to me, "I'm your sweet child; Jim is your smart one."

But I never said that—maybe his aunt Ella did, never realizing the effect it might have on Paul.

Elmer purchased the family home on Mount Overlook back in 1914, before the neighborhood was built up. We were one of the only black families there. Eventually new houses on Mount Overlook brought new people. Just before the Second World War, some people were not allowed to live where they wanted, or to buy in certain areas. I disapproved of that.

We never had trouble. Elmer hadn't moved to the area initially to get away from anyone; he got a good price on a house for his family then coming up from the South. Later, after he got sick and couldn't go out, one of the neighbors stayed near the window and could see Elmer seated at the table where he had his book. They liked him. They didn't want that relationship disturbed. Elmer and I didn't worry about our relationship with the neighbors, because over the years we'd all meet and stop and talk. We'd go into their house or they'd come into mine, and the children played together. On Mount Overlook, most of the children were Italian or northern European. They went to the Catholic Church, and we went to the Protestant. That's how it was. I didn't make a big deal out of being in the neighborhood as the boys grew up. It was a neighborhood of upward strivers; everybody was trying to make their way, whether they were Italian, northern European, or whatever. Most of them came because they wanted a better home or a better job or a better life for their children.

But when Jim entered school, the Anthony Wayne Elementary School, he was one of the few Negroes, or whatever we were. He came home one day and he said, "I don't like my name; I don't like Cheeks."

I said, "Why?"

He said, "All the little boys are named Angelo, or some other Italian names, and I don't like not being like them."

I told him, "Honey, you have to be there with them because that's who you are." I didn't visit the school often; I was working and I had another child. But in the end, Jim managed to do very well as a student.

My husband had provided for his family. He left two insurance policies: the one I cashed in a few years after his death; and another one that ran for ten years, giving Jim a hundred dollars a month for expenses while he was in college. Jim didn't get financial help from the University of Chicago. He got the placement, and the acceptance, and the opportunity. But I had to pay the tuition.

Jim graduated from the University of Chicago with

his first degree, and later he got a law degree also. He then served in the army, mostly in Germany, where he worked in the office of the adjutant general. He was stationed in Heidelberg, headquarters of the U.S. Army in Europe, between 1954 and 1956. Paul completed his service stateside.

Jim says: "I think gratefully of my mother's financial sacrifice to support me in college. She and my father were both driven to get an education and leave the South. When they met in Cleveland, each saw in the other one who had worked hard to achieve the goals they shared. They had sons, whose education they planned for, proud that they could make greater provision for their children than had been made for them. The college fund they were building at my father's early death would not have been enough. But my mother generously supported, out of now-diminished family income, the college education of sons who would meet her condition to take education seriously and work at it."

Though a hundred dollars a month for Jim was a lot of money then, costs at the university ate it up. I used what I earned to pay his school costs; but in 1942, I also bought another house, a two-family house in the Glenville neighborhood, as an investment. I didn't know anything about real estate and how to get this done. But I had two friends who did, Mr. J. Walter Wills and Herman Storey. When I was going to settle the procedure with the man who owned the house on Tacoma in Glenville, I said, "Herman, I want you to go with me when I meet with them and their lawyer, because I can't be sure I'll hear what I want to hear."

He came. When he left, he said, "You didn't need me. You asked all the right questions."

I guess I'd learned the lessons of our commencement speaker at Fisk: "You don't need to know everything, but you need to know where to get the information."

At a certain point in time, I decided to move into this rental property in Glenville. Given that it was a two-family house, we could live in one part and gain some income by renting out the other. In Glenville we had friends and relatives who could look after Paul when I was at work. We had a housekeeper who took care of the boys, and if for some reason she couldn't come, Ella Phillips, Elmer's sister and the wife of our pastor, lived just two blocks away; Jim and Paul could just walk around to Ella's house.

We were a bit isolated on Mount Overlook. Glenville

was a more populous area, with much more commercial activity, that had been settled by many African Americans in the 1930s as the Jewish population began to move out to the surrounding suburbs. My church, Mt. Zion, actually purchased a former Jewish temple there to convert to a church. But they lost it in financial difficulties and later bought the property in University Circle, where the church is still located, in what was once a YWCA.

Even after I went ahead and bought the house in Glenville, I kept the one on Mount Overlook, renting it out because Jim and Paul didn't want to break their ties to their first home. Though Paul especially objected to leaving his friends on Mount Overlook, we went ahead and moved into the lower apartment of the two-family house in Glenville. I rented the upstairs. Now I had two rentals, including the property we'd left behind.

I didn't do much gardening when I moved to Glenville. I didn't have a garden at all, because I had a two-story house; and with no husband to work with, I couldn't manage it. We lived in this house in Glenville for about three years until we moved back into the original family home on Mount Overlook in 1945, after World War II had ended. Fourteen at the time, Jim was satisfied with playing his records and reading the books of his choice—he could entertain himself—but he didn't want to stay away from his first home. That's where his father died.

The woman who had rented the house on Mount Overlook after we moved to Glenville felt she'd done nothing to justify being evicted. I gave her time, two or three months, to find a new place. When I told her she had to leave, she said, "I'm protected . . ."

During the war, landlords couldn't just summarily evict a tenant unless there was cause. She wasn't belligerent. She was speaking her mind, which she should have. She told me, "You can't move me unless you're planning to live there."

I said, "That's it. We plan to move back."

My sons wanted to return to the original family home and I didn't object. This was where I had spent years with Elmer. I loved my home. I loved my family. And I'd always liked the neighbors.

Once the boys were just about grown and would soon be moving out, I decided to make my single-family house on Mount Overlook into a two-family, to generate rental income once again.

As Paul relates it, "A contractor was contacted and, after many long meetings during which various cost estimates were submitted, a final contract was prepared for my mother's signature.

"Sitting at the kitchen table, the contractor took out his pen and stated, 'Here, Ella Mae, why don't you use my pen?'

"Mom's back straightened. She looked him in the eye and announced, 'You do not know me well enough to call me Ella Mae; I will not be signing this contract.'"

Another contractor was found and eventually the work was completed; but not without some resistance from neighbors.

The house had started out with two bedrooms and a bath on the second floor, and a kitchen, dining room, living room, and one bedroom on the first floor. But we'd added another bedroom and a bathroom on the first floor so Elmer wouldn't have to climb the steps. The only time he had to climb the steps was when he came in or went out of the house.

I wasn't increasing the house in terms of square footage. I was reducing the size of the first-floor bathroom and the kitchen. I wanted to put two sets of rooms together: the living-dining room, and two of the second-floor bedrooms. Before Elmer died, we'd finished the third floor for Jim.

There was a man from southern Europe, from Italy, who had moved into the house three doors down from ours. This man had come and secured work and bought a house. He was ready to bring his family, but he couldn't because of the new immigration quotas instituted after the war.

When you wanted to do housing changes in Cleveland, you had to urge or invite the neighbors to come to meetings about the zoning laws. The Italian man who bought the house near mine started talking to some of the neighbors after I applied to alter my home.

He said, "I disapprove." He told some of the neighbors who had been there for years, "I am going to the meeting to speak against her changing her house." Some of the neighbors he spoke to knew how long I had been there, long before most of the houses there had even been built. The message I sent out to them was, "You know me; you know the way I live. If he succeeds in blocking me, I'll sell to the highest bidder, and it won't matter to me whether you like them or not."

So they didn't go to the meeting. When he got there, he didn't have enough people who saw things from his perspective, to vote his way. We had no trouble. To me he was implying he had higher standards than I had! I didn't think so. That was the end of that.

After Elmer died, my social life revolved mostly around church events; between my job and taking care of my two sons, I had very little spare time. At Mt. Zion, I became acquainted with Raymond Johnson, an officer of the Probation Department of the Cleveland Municipal Court. He was married to a friend of mine, Wilberetta Pope Johnson, an accomplished woman who was the first assistant principal of color in the Cleveland schools. She was also a sorority sister in Alpha Kappa Alpha.

At a certain point after Wilberetta passed away, Ray started coming to visit me, which I didn't consider "dating," per se. I didn't say he ought to come to see me. But he was responsive, and had no wife then. I trusted his judgment and he trusted mine. When you're in your fifties or sixties, it's all more subtle. Ray was kind, patient, and very considerate. He was a gentle man, rather quiet but very, very supportive of me. Though Ray wasn't necessarily interested in everything I was, we had things in common. I was a social worker, and he was a probation officer. We both worked with people. Our social circles overlapped.

After I accepted Ray's offer of marriage, a friend asked, "What do your boys think?"

I said, "I never asked what they thought." When Jim and Paul got married, they didn't need my help. Nor did I ask for theirs. I don't think they expected me to ask them what they thought; I could decide for myself. I purposely didn't marry until both of them were out of college. I was fifty-three when Ray and I got married in 1957, in a small family ceremony at Mt. Zion conducted by Rev. Richard Andrews. It was followed by a reception in the church's social hall.

I was Ray's third wife. His first wife, Ruth Wright, was the mother of his son, Wright Johnson, who'd been given her family name. Her sister Bea Wright Fox was a dear friend of mine. Ray and Wright lived together in a home with other family members after Ruth died. There was kind of an extended family network in those days that took care of people when someone passed on. About ten years after Ruth died, Ray married Wilberetta.

I didn't start my new married life as an eighteen-year-old. Twice married before, Ray knew what his goal was, and I knew mine; we worked things out together. If I chose to buy this instead of that, or if we chose together, and were satisfied, well, that was that.

He was enterprising. Ray worked hard and concentrated on achieving his goals. He owned an apartment building with twenty-two units. Once there was a tenant with a leaky faucet in the bathroom, and after he reported it, Ray got out of the house and went over. Another time a similar problem came up at 1:00 a.m. Ray got up and got dressed. He was a hard worker, and a good businessman. His son and his family lived in one of the apartments in his building. One day the son thought his father should not expect any rent from him; but that wasn't Ray's way. If he was going to give it to you, he gave it to you. He didn't give it to you because he thought you expected it.

He was ambitious, and industrious, and he was generous—with his family, with the church, with his fraternity, and in his YMCA activities. He was on the board of the Cedar YMCA and active in the youth programs there. And, of course, as a probation officer he was giving advice to the men and boys who needed guidance about the right things to do in their lives.

Ray was slightly older than me, by perhaps two years.

He was born in Cleveland. So few of us were. Most people had come from the South. Ray was born in the area near Shaker Heights and Shaker Boulevard, the youngest of eight children. Two of his older siblings were involved with postal work, and two sisters became public school teachers. Since he was the youngest in this large family, he was watched over by one sister in particular, Emma Stevenson, the oldest, who helped raise Ray. They had a bond, because Emma took care of him. In good times or bad times, he'd talk with her. Every day, Ray called Emma. That continued until the day she died.

He'd say, "Emma, I want you to know what happened to me today." I don't think he felt she *had* to know. But he wanted her to know. If he didn't telephone her, she telephoned him. I didn't question it or regard her as intrusive. She was his sister, and in my mind, she had acted as a mother to Ray. In the years Ray and I were together, I wanted to share with her the things that were important to him.

Ray attended public schools and went one year to Howard University, where he got involved with Army ROTC. During World War II, he was encouraged, as others were, to sign up. The ROTC service was counted into the service requirements then. When Ray was of the age and place to be eligible for Social Security, he was eligible not only for certain benefits for himself; he could also choose to direct part of his income to include me, because of his military service. Teachers, preachers, social workers, and public servants didn't immediately qualify. As a social worker, I didn't qualify on my own for retirement benefits.

Some social workers felt it was beneath them to protest. When I say "protest," I mean to demand. I think they mistakenly thought that as teachers or social workers or whatever we were, we ought to be able to get it without forcing it. The unions, which initiated many, many strikes, ended up helping some people who would not follow the union line, and hadn't fought for it.

Later the state made some decisions about ways their workers could qualify. There was a teachers' pension fund. There was a social workers' fund. At first, Elmer wasn't qualified. The program that would later include him started so late that he got very little pension. It was so small that he didn't share it with me. Ray did. Things were different then. I couldn't prove when I was born; on my own, I never qualified for Social Security. But Ray arranged to share what would come to him with me, and so that's how I could go to the hospital or the doctor and share its cost. Not because of what I did, but because I was married to someone who shared his.

Our home on Pasadena Avenue allowed us to entertain more people than I had on Mount Overlook. We had what we called "the social hall" in the basement, large enough to accommodate ten folding tables for bridge games. I became "Nan" to Ray's son, Wright, Wright's wife, Juanita, and their daughter, Ruth, as well as a grandmother to Ruth's two children, Robert and Renee Taylor.

For her first five years, Jim's daughter, Audrey, came to live with me and Raymond. It was a joy to have her.

Audrey remembers: "As a child living with Ella Mae and Ray, I would sit in the front seat with them when we took drives in Grandpa's Lincoln. On one occasion, I asked Grandma to sit in the back with me as we drove—I don't remember why. She explained that she couldn't do this because people would assume Grandpa was our chauffeur. Not being race-conscious at all at that time—not even realizing that I was of mixed race—this did not occur to me, nor did the fact that such as an assumption would hurt him or anyone else. This is an example of how Ella Mae both demonstrated empathy and taught me a lesson in sensitivity growing up.

"At another time, I recall that we were at the home of

Ray's beloved sister Emma. Given that there being no children around (as one might expect when being raised as a preschooler by grandparents), I became bored and wanted to leave. My grandmother very calmly reminded me of Ray's tireless efforts to please me. In return, she suggested, on this occasion I could defer my wishes (in this case, to get home to watch *The Flintstones*).

"Looking back on this, I'm again struck by her thoughtfulness, her sense of fairness, and her respect for me, even as she disciplined me (in the original sense of the word). She didn't simply lay down the law as a parent might have in her position of authority; she presented me with a perspective about the situation and gave me the opportunity to make a decision. That kind of parenting takes longer and requires more effort, but she clearly believed it was worth the effort. As I remember, it was effective."

When Audrey first came to live with us, Ray had asked me, "As soon as we fall in love with her, will we have to send her back?" When she was of school age, Audrey did return to New York to live with her parents. Eventually she made her way to Stanford. She still lives in California, where she works with computers. She has two children, Nika Wehba, who just graduated from UC

Santa Barbara, and Andrew Wehba, a student at UC Davis.

My grandsons are George and Jimmy, sons of Paul. A graduate of Yale and Harvard Law School, George is in Manhattan, like his uncle Jim. He's executive vice president and co–general counsel at MTV.

Now forty-four years old, George Cheeks remembers: "Grandma always placed the highest priority on education. She told me that I would only be able to achieve my potential if I studied hard and truly appreciated the value of an education. My first year at college was a difficult one. In addition to the ordinary transition issues a first year student faces, my father was going through an especially difficult time personally, professionally, and financially. About halfway through the academic year, it was apparent that my dad would be unable to cover the tuition costs for the balance of the year. I was devastated, as I finally had found momentum and direction and the last thing I wanted to do was stop midstream in my first year. Even though it was not easy for her given that she had to carefully monitor 'cash out,' Grandma stepped in right away and covered the cost for the balance of the year. When she told me what she planned to do, she looked me in the eye and said that she was doing it because she loved me and she wanted me to continue to work hard and succeed. I felt so incredibly grateful to her. Whenever I felt like slacking off after that, I thought about the sacrifice she had made for me and it snapped me right back in line."

I am also great-grandmother to Alex and Nicholas, the young sons of Jimmy, who has a home-building business, and his wife, Wendy, who live in Atlanta.

Jimmy Cheeks, forty-one, describes his visits to see his grandmother: "I am so in awe of Ella Mae Johnson. For the last fifteen years or so I have made a point to spend as much time with her as possible out of desire, not obligation. We sit and talk for a few hours about politics, family, my work, her church.

"My grandma is not a frivolous woman. She didn't necessarily agree with many aspects of how my parents raised George and me. She was never indulgent, but was very willing to help us further our career paths. In middle school I was very interested in becoming a dolphin trainer at SeaWorld. As you can imagine, that may not have seemed a wise career path to her way of thinking. But she saw me remain focused (and I didn't have much of that in middle school); so she searched out her own way to help me. In the back of the Sunday *New York Times Magazine* was an advertisement for Sea Camp in the Florida Keys. The camp had a significant impact on me, and eventually I became a dolphin trainer at Sea-World. Grandma was focused on helping us grow and learn even though she may not have thought I was making the right career choice."

CHAPTER SIX

TO PRAY AND PRAISE: A SEEKER'S JOURNEY

Let Us Cheer the Weary Traveler

—TRADITIONAL SPIRITUAL

When I retired in 1961, I began my travels in earnest. Travel has been a privilege and a blessing because of my interest in the needs and welfare of people abroad as well as at home. I actually started traveling in 1954, on a tour organized to Mexico and the Panama Canal by the Phillis Wheatley Association, a multiservice community center where I served on the board.

I decided I wanted to go to the Holy Land. I had read about it. It had been a part of history, of tradition at Fisk, to read the Psalms and the Scriptures as well as to sing spirituals. I took a three-week trip in 1956, a religious tour led by Harriet-Louise H. Patterson, author of *Come with Me to the Holy Land*, that included Egypt, Greece, Jordan, Bethlehem, and Jerusalem, where we spent Easter. Israel was a newly formed country then.

We stopped in Rome on the way there and then again on the way home.

In my earliest travels, I took pictures with a box camera. Many of my first trips were tied up with my spiritual beliefs. Much earlier Elmer's sister Ella Phillips had advised me, "If you're going to travel, have it mean something. As long as it doesn't disturb other people, do what you want to do."

On trips I'd taken people would buy this-and-this-and-this, to take home and show. I said, "I don't need to prove to anyone that I've been to Texas or whatever place." Nor did I need to spend a lot of money. I just wanted to see the wider world, and think about my place in it. When I look back over the course of my life, I realize I never had a master plan; I let the Master plan.

Growing up, I was a seeker. I wanted to know what Christ wanted of me. How did I know what He wanted me to do—and how would He tell me how to do it? I endured by seeing what people said, older than I and more experienced—how they lived as Christians. That didn't mean that I disregarded people who were not Christians. That didn't mean that everything that the Davises did was Christian, necessarily. But I started from there. I need so much to be able to live according to my beliefs.

Though I read the Bible, I also read interesting and inspiring books and other material. I appreciated the Bible study groups when I was able to attend them. I prefer the Socratic way within a study group, not just lectures. I want to hear and discuss what the Bible means to others.

When I went to the Holy Land again in 1966, it was with a group led by a female minister who had graduated from a school of theology, but couldn't find a church that would take a female pastor. So she decided that instead of leading a congregation, she would take people to the Holy Land. She gave us instructions about what happened there before and during Christ's day—the beginning of the Judeo-Christian connection. As we left Kennedy Airport, she prayed that our group, departing as tourists, would return as pilgrims. Though my husband Ray didn't accompany me on these trips, he was very supportive of my travels overall.

I could, and did, walk where Jesus had. I could visit the places where He lived, served, died, and was resurrected. Every day on the tour, I would look at the schedule, then at the Scripture, and say, "Let's see, why do I want to go there?"

In the Holy Land, I used my Bible, my hymnal, and the material the leader of the trip provided. I read the Scripture at the end of each day, and I prayed for understanding. I don't boast that I'm a Christian, but I acknowledge it totally. I'm not a perfect person; I make mistakes. I misunderstand. But I want to do the best I can.

On our trip, I didn't want to go to one place or another just to tell people I'd done so. So when I looked over the minister's material, and the Bible, I'd ask myself: "What did I do yesterday? Why did I go to that place? What did I get out of it?"

I'd do that at night, and in the morning, I'd take it again and say, "This is where I'm going today. Why?"

Sometimes our tour leader would talk to me alone about the Bible, because I would ask her questions. I told her about the Fisk Glee Club—about the spirituals we sang. I can say with all sincerity that going to the Holy Land taught me what my religion meant to me. I could now sing "I Walked Today Where Jesus Walked" and recall this experience of experiences.

At Fisk, we'd sung, "Go down Moses, and tell old Pharaoh to let my people go." We weren't slaves when we sang these words; it was the Jews who'd been enslaved in ancient times. When we were singing, "Joshua fit the Battle of Jericho," it was in dialect; the words should have been "Joshua fought the battle." It may not have been totally grammatical, but the spirit was in it.

It seemed that some people frowned on the fact that I didn't pick up the Bible to say, "Here it is, this is what I've got to do," because the pastor or the leaders read it that way. I wanted to see how it came to me, and to make my own path. I went to Damascus, in Syria. I went to Lebanon. I went to many of the countries listed in the Bible as fact. And if I didn't understand it, I would ask someone else. As I traveled around the Middle East, I often heard, "This saying is a tradition," meaning they couldn't guarantee it, but that an event likely occurred in the general vicinity. I didn't worry about whether or not certain things had actually happened there. What impressed me and what encouraged me was that they had happened.

In Bethlehem, I looked over what they called the mountain; I think the Scripture said it was the hills. Then I went down the road where according to tradition, the man was beaten and then rescued by the Good Samaritan. As the story of the Good Samaritan goes, a young lawyer asked Jesus, "What shall I do to inherit eternal life?"

When Jesus asked him what the law said, the man responded: "Thou shalt love the Lord with all thy heart, all thy soul, all thy strength, and all thy mind, and thy neighbor as thyself."

He told the lawyer a parable: A certain man went down from Jerusalem to Jericho and fell among thieves who robbed him, stripped him of his clothing, and beat him and left him for dead. A priest and separately a Levite saw him and crossed to the other side. In contrast, a Samaritan saw the man and took pity on him. He cleaned and bound his wounds, placed him on his donkey, and took him to an inn, where he engaged the innkeeper to take care of him, saying he would be paid no matter what the cost.

Jesus didn't always come through with a lot of explanation. It just was. There are so many things like that in the Bible. In this case, the message of compassion was clear, and has always inspired me as I seek to know what God wants me to be and do.

I went ahead to Egypt, to the Nile River where Moses had been placed by his sister, Miriam. Pharaoh's daughter found the baby in a basket in the bulrushes, and he was raised as royalty. Eventually Moses became the one anointed to lead his people out of slavery. He did not get to go all the way, because he had been a sinner earlier in his life, disobeying the word of the Lord, and according to some accounts, murdering an abusive Egyptian taskmaster. So the Bible says he was denied the opportunity to go into the Promised Land. I visited Mount Nebo, where Moses stayed while the other Israelites went over the mountain.

On the night before his death, Martin Luther King Jr. referred to it symbolically: "I've been to the mountain top, and I've looked over and seen the Promised Land." King added, "I may not get there," but he did not let that stop him. And he didn't limit his comments to people of one race. He said, "Freedom for all men." There are people who want to get tied up on whether he meant women, too. But terminology isn't the thing that's important; the meaning is.

In the Holy Land, I visited Nazareth, Capernaum, Bethlehem, the Mountains of Temptation, the Jordan River, Cana, Jericho, the Garden of Gethsemane, Samaria, the Via Dolorosa, the Judean Wilderness, and the Sea of Galilee, among other places where Jesus walked and lived. Some years after I took my trip, I said to my pastor, Dr. F. Allison Phillips: "You have to go to the Holy Land. You have to see and feel it. You are a pastor. You're a minister. You're a teacher. Go and see what that means to you. You'll never feel the same."

After he came back, he told me, "You told me that after I went to the Holy Land, I'd never be the same. I'm not!"

For me, there is nothing more important than a broad vision of the world. That's why we travel. In the Holy Land, I went to one or two mosques or synagogues, but if you weren't a member of that religion, you were limited in where you could go on their property. Sometimes people not of that faith were allowed in at certain times.

I was comfortable praying in Jewish synagogues in Damascus, Syria; Cairo, Egypt; and in Israel; in mosques in Addis Abba, Ethiopia, and the Dome of the Rock in Jerusalem; at the Bahai Shrine in Haifa, Israel; at a Japanese shrine outside Tokyo; and to the goddesses Diana and Helena near Athens, Greece. I've gone into Coptic churches in Egypt, including Abu Sarga, said to stand over the site of the Holy Family's home; the Church of the Nativity in Bethlehem; the church over the site in

Damascus, Syria, where Saul lived following his conversion; the Church of the Holy Sepulchre in Jerusalem; Our Lady of Guadelupe in Mexico City; and St. Paul Outside the Walls as well as St. Peter's Basilica in Rome. When I hear things like, "This is not like my church," or "This isn't right," and "This isn't the correct thing," I am not impressed.

As Colin Powell said when people claimed Barack Obama was a Muslim: "So what?"

My beliefs define me, but that doesn't mean I can't respect those of others. In a discussion of spiritual issues, I don't have to accept what you think; but I will respect your right to go your own way.

If my pastor said something from the pulpit I didn't agree with, I might take it under advisement and then quietly go my own way. I would never embarrass him. If he believes something, or his wife does, and I believe something else, fine by me. They have a right to their thoughts and beliefs. But when I pray, it's between God and me; I don't need anyone in between us.

I wouldn't be Ella Mae if I did what I don't believe. That's part of my faith and my hope.

Some years ago, we were in what we call Reflections

class. One of the members asked the pastor who was leading the discussion about the Creation of the world: "What do you believe about the Creation story?"

This pastor turned and asked all of us: "What do *you* think about it?"

Some people don't want you to know. They really don't want you to seem to be competing with them. When it was my turn, I said, "I don't know what I believe about it, but I will pray, and maybe God will lead me."

Who is your God? If someone asks me which denomination I prefer, I choose Congregationalism, which to me means the democratic way. Since 1926, that method has been my choice, because I am able to express my thoughts and still take in those of others. I believe God wants to hear everyone's thoughts.

I have a letter from my grandson Jimmy, quoting from remarks he made at a birthday party. He said, "My grandmother never told me that I should go to church. She told me to learn about all religions, and then decide later whether or not I liked any of them."

Jimmy Cheeks adds: "Though Grandma is a very religious and spiritual person, her relationship with God is very private. She knew that George and I were baptized Greek Orthodox, which was our mother's faith;

but growing up we were not very religious. She could tell that as a young man I had my doubts. But instead of trying to instill her beliefs in me, she simply asked that I learn as much as possible about all the various religions and come to my own conclusions. She clearly had a defined opinion, but did everything possible to encourage rather than to dictate."

I believe in asking, listening, and allowing people to come to their own judgments. I'm not in favor of what you'd call top-down religion. I've volunteered at Mt. Zion Church and served on all levels of the board of the United Church of Christ.

Things change gradually. We'll never get it right if we don't acknowledge mistakes along the way, something President Obama understands. I'm hoping if we do things or we don't do them, someone will acknowledge, "We didn't do that right; let's correct it." But know that you can't correct it by yourself. History is important, and so is seeing the world, so we can know the many mistakes made by mankind.

Traveling also teaches self-reliance. Once on a trip to Switzerland in the late 1950s, I became separated from the rest of the group in Zurich, where we'd gone because it was the headquarters of the United Church of Christ.

Some of our mission funds went there. I looked around and it was just beautiful. I remember buildings that looked like they might slide down the mountain. From where we were, they appeared to be very, very small.

I said to the leader, "This doesn't look like a place where they need mission funds."

She said, "No, but there are some of us who wanted to come because the Reform Church was founded here." The Reform Church and two or three churches had joined to make the United Church of Christ.

As we stopped at the main church, I paused to put some film in my camera. When I looked up, everyone was gone. I couldn't speak the language of the people walking past, and I saw no one who could speak mine. I couldn't figure out where the rest of the group was. After wandering around for a while, I remembered that I had gone to a certain place to buy something, and had taken the bus there to make the purchase. I determined to retrace my steps and go the same way. Eventually I wound up back in the place where we were staying.

I got there before the group did. So I wrote a note and left it at the desk: "We got separated. In fact, you got lost, and I've come home."

Of course, I got lost again during the course of this

trip. Some of them were worried about me: "What about Ella Mae?"

A friend of mine said, "You don't need to worry; you know what she did before." Life is interesting when you know how to "make do."

For this journey, Ray kept a copy of the itinerary. He sent me a letter saying, "I need a watch." Switzerland is the place to buy watches and clocks and things. And Ray liked to buy quality.

He didn't lose his watch. What happened was that there was a man who came along the street while Ray was working out in the yard. He kept his yard and his flowers and everything up-to-date to the season. This man admired Ray's handiwork. So Ray said, "Come into my house; I want you to see my home." Ray took him to see the interior of the house. When that man left, Ray's watch went, too. Things just happen, one thing to another.

In 1973, I went to Kenya ten years after colonization had ended, accompanying delegates of the United Church of Christ's Board for World Ministries. My interest in the African subcontinent dated all the way back to 1925, when I met Mr. and Mrs. McDowell, an African American couple who were Congregational Church missionaries on leave from assignment in Africa. In Kenya, I met a young man nearly consumed with his hopes for his country, and the part he might play in it. He had heard of the interest some African Americans took in their heritage—the customs and culture, the food and fabrics, the music and dance. He knew many named their children African names. He considered them part of a larger extended family.

But by the time I met him in 1973, his bubble had burst. When African Americans visited on tour, they treated their African hosts as inferiors, haggling over prices and being arrogant and demanding, in his view. In my outreach, perhaps I was trying to compensate him for his obvious pain. Though I didn't keep in touch with him personally, I followed stories in the news about that country in the years after I visited. And I continue to beg members of my church to contribute to United Nations efforts in Kenya to supply safe drinking water as well as food and medical care.

Africa—that's approximately the beginning of civilization. Oh, how many troubles they've had. They were colonies primarily of the British, and then others all over Europe. Once you have power, you're going to fight to keep it, especially after World War II, when people had gotten together and tried to decide who was going to run this country and that one. That's when it all started. By their actions people announced, "You are not my equal, I can rule you"—and sadly, some of their own people treated the people as badly as their colonizers had. So that's the Africa I remember.

I went to Africa with my church group not just because I wanted to, but because I wanted to know how these people survived. I didn't go there to impose my view, to say, "This is what you ought to do." I wanted to know what they thought about themselves. But I looked, and I saw where there was no equality. There seemed to be little progress. It was at least as bad as when these countries were colonies. I went to Egypt, and to Ethiopia, to consider the stories of the people. They became like we had been in this country: beholden, unsure, having to do what other people said, suffering physical and mental problems as a result.

In fact, when we went to Ethiopia and were sitting at dinner, one of the native people said, "Don't discuss the situation here now; we're having trouble." The country had been occupied by Italy during the Mussolini years, in the 1930s; perhaps there were ongoing problems after the Ethiopians fought their way out of it. They may also have been having difficulties with neighboring Eritrea.

We didn't discuss politics that night; there was trouble, as there has always been trouble, and will continue to be. Prayer isn't the sole answer. If it were, then we would have prayed, and it wouldn't have come.

More recently, I went to Ghana, my last trip out of the United States in 1974. I was intrigued that Du Bois had given up his American citizenship and is buried in Ghana. He gave up because he so completely rejected the way the United States was doing things, not just to his people, but elsewhere. After leaning to the Left for a number of years, he'd been indicted in the 1950s as an agent "of foreign powers," namely Russia. Even though he was acquitted, he left the country. When I was in Accra, Ghana, I found the street named for Du Bois.

Over the years, I traveled to five of seven continents and in this way saw the world anew. I marveled at the beauty of a silvery streak of light at sunrise over the Atlantic and over the Nile River in Cairo; the gloriously orange sunset over the Mediterranean from Beirut; the Haleakala volcano in Hawaii, a trip that also included stops in the Philippines and Japan; the game preserve in the Serengeti, with its thundering herds of animals and its beautiful, stately Masai tribes in Kenya; the Swiss Alps, near Zurich; the Andes mountains outside Caracas,

Venezuela; Mount Kilimanjaro, near Kenya's border; the California Redwood forests, whose trees seem to touch the heavens; the Grand Canyon; the cascading waters of Niagara Falls; and the ethereal and lovely Acropolis in Athens, which appeared suspended in the sky. In awe I offered prayers while there, and since. I saw the different nationalities and races of people whom He would have live peaceably together, all created by Him and in his Image.

I was so inspired by the example of Lillian Carter, who joined the Peace Corps, a sixty-eight-year-old registered nurse, and worked in a clinic in India. She was a real "Good Samaritan," whose story was told by her son Jimmy Carter in one of his books.

In 1966, I worshiped alone in Jerusalem on Easter morning, overlooking the Kidron Valley and the Golden Gate. I would love to go back to the Holy Land again.

In Accra, Ghana, in 1973, I said in English what the Ghanaian congregation sang in their language: *"It is well with my soul."* So it is!

I declare to Him, "How Great Thou Art," over and over again. Praise to the Creator is the only possible response to the sights I've seen, despite the troubles the whole world knows.

CHAPTER SEVEN

AGING SUCCESSFULLY

I will lift up mine eyes unto the hills,
from whence cometh my help.
My help cometh from the Lord,
which made heaven and earth.

—PSALM 121:1–2

I've been living at Judson Park for thirty-four years. My second husband, Raymond Johnson, and I moved in 1975 to Judson's high-rise apartments, encouraged by a friend named Selma Palmer, who advised me that Judson had long-life care for residents should they need it later. Ray didn't want to keep maintaining the house and the yard. In addition, our tenant had been burglarized; we didn't want that responsibility anymore.

In the high-rise, we entertained church members and family and had an active life. After Ray became ill, I learned to drive at age seventy. To get a driver's license at that age, I had to prove, as well as I could, that I was capable. Both of my husbands did the shopping; they did everything you needed a car for. If I had to go somewhere, if I had to go to church with Elmer, he would take me and leave me there. Soon after I married Ray, his health worsened. He got to the point that he couldn't do the shopping and had to go to the Cleveland Clinic. He went so often that his son said that his father was paying for part of the building.

One day when I was learning to drive, and was going this way and that way, Ray started to ask, "Why didn't you turn that way, when the sign said to do so?"

I didn't argue with him. I just got out of the car and walked away. If he was going to keep picking on me, I was going to have an accident. He didn't fight it. He didn't argue about it. He wanted me to learn but in due course, if that's what it took to make me safe on the roads.

By the time I was eighty, I stopped driving; I felt I'd be risking somebody else's life, and mine, if I stayed on the road. If I made a mistake and put my foot on the pedal when it should have been taken off, someone might have died. I didn't want to be responsible for some other family's suffering. So I went back to taking a taxi or accepting a friend's offer of a ride.

Driving for ten years enabled me to stay active in community affairs. I served as president of the Board of Trustees of the Phillis Wheatley Association, founded by a prominent social worker, Jane Edna Hunter, the daughter of a sharecropper who trained at Hampton in Virginia as a nurse and then came north when many other African Americans were also doing so. We wanted to leave Jim Crow and its limitations and legacy behind.

Eventually Jane Hunter also passed the bar in Ohio; and in 1911, she started the Working Girls Association in Cleveland to provide safe living quarters for African American women, to teach them skills so that they could work at being housekeepers and cooks, or whatever they desired. People were looking for a chance for a better life then—better education, better health care. So those types of organizations were built. Later it became the Phillis Wheatley Association, named for a remarkably accomplished African woman who was brought to America as a slave in the eighteenth century and became a well-known poet of the day.

When $150 was needed for repairs to the plaster, paint, and fixtures in the ladies' room at the Wheatley Association, I knitted an afghan and auctioned it off to raise money. The room was unofficially dubbed "the Johnson john" by Cheryle Wills, who oversaw donations from the House of Wills, the funeral home that had aided my client Christine Buster in getting to Ohio State. I was also cochairman of the Alpha Kappa Alpha Sorority Job Corps Committee and Chairman of the Women's Fellowships Friendly Town Program, both intended to help the needy. Friends like Pallie Hunter were there to help when I asked for assistance for Christmas gifts for Job Corps or a donation for Friendly Town.

In the late sixties, the federal government had set up a program to give young men and women who'd dropped out of school "a second chance." My good friend Zelma George became head of the Cleveland Job Corps Center. The local chapter of AKA was put in charge of the center; that's how closely the sorority involved itself in community affairs. Some of us did a form of mentoring, in which a sorority member, or "soror," was matched with a young woman to encourage her in her interests. My husband Ray joined me in meeting three young women. One was a hard worker and a good mixer who interacted well with both men and women and would have succeeded in any career she chose. The second, a Mexican American, was interested in everything we planned for and with her. But we had no success with the third young woman, who was never ready when we arrived, and seemed totally disengaged. Sadly, she was no doubt the neediest of the three; but our time together didn't allow us to establish a rapport.

A few years ago when I was 102, I was honored with the "Diamond Diva" award from AKA for so many years of community service.

In programs at Judson, which has a well-stocked crafts center, I would make things, and paint and knit and crochet to get extra money—primarily to help, whether it was an individual or community activity. I loved to weave. But I had to stop because my hands don't work any more; and I couldn't see how to run the thread into the loom. I'd been making things since I was a little girl. During the First World War, I was in a group in school asked to make khaki-colored scarves for the soldiers. We knitted them in class. I was about ten at the time. That's when I began working with my hands to help others.

During retirement I sang in a choir. I taught Sunday school. I worked in a gift shop. I baked cookies, which were sold—though I wasn't known as a good cook. But the cookies were special because after they were sold, most of the money went to those in need. All these activities helped me not to buy another dress, but enabled me to do things for other people. That's what God wants me to do. It helped me make my way after Raymond Johnson died in 1983.

When I was eighty, I was diagnosed with breast cancer. I'd discovered the lump by accident one day when I reached down because I thought I'd dropped something. So I went to see a nurse at Judson. Then I talked to the doctor, who then consulted with a surgeon. I went into St. Luke's Hospital. Within about a week or so after I discovered the lump, the surgery was performed. My son Jim had been on his way to Hawaii when I notified him. I said, "Don't worry, I'll be out." He went on his trip but came to see me as soon as he got back.

There was a constant stream of people in my room at the hospital. I asked my doctor, "What in the world is going on?" He explained that the other medical people were surprised someone my age had done so well with that type surgery, a mastectomy. For a follow-up treatment, I tried a new type that didn't make me lose my hair. I never had a recurrence of the cancer.

My family and friends help by contributing to the needy instead of giving me personal gifts on my birthdays. Of course, I don't earn money today. But I'm not starving. I have what I need, and in many instances, just what I want.

Some people might say, Ella Mae, now that you've reached 106, what do you think about when you get up in the morning? Do you look forward? Do you look back? How do you greet each day?

I wake up and often I look at the painting of the Good Samaritan. In terms of what I've done lately, I think: "Was that compassionate? Did that help anybody? Could I do something different?" Compassion means everything to me. It's within me. It's been within me since as a four-year-old I was taken care of by someone other than my biological family. It started in 1908, when my mother died.

I don't know what I am. I am black, or at least no longer colored. I am African American. Even if people called me "nigger" or "Negro" or whatever, I know *who* I am; so why should I worry about them calling me something I don't like? Nonetheless, there is something about being African American that should be special, that should enable me to feel more sympathetic, to understand, or attempt to understand, more kinds of people.

Sometime between the two world wars, I sent a gift to the Armenians, who were in trouble. A young man working in the downtown office of the relief agency called me and said that he had received the check, and mailed it; but he said he was "surprised, because we don't have diplomatic relations with Armenia."

It never mattered to me. Unless it was illegal, I would help the needy.

The young man was very politically minded; but I explained to him that I wanted to send it because of the need. Politics had nothing to do with it. All people, no matter their religion or race or country of origin, have needs.

When I first moved to Judson Park there were two women beginning to be my friends. One worked with me and lived in the Judson Manor. This was a time when sincere whites were trying to understand how to get along with black people. They wondered, "How do I understand them? She is black. She may want something else."

"What should I call you?" they asked me.

I said, "I don't care what you call me, as long as you respect me." Though they had not mistreated me, this was my answer to them. They never embarrassed me. In fact, they embraced me.

There are many ways to form bonds with people, and sometimes you just say, "Okay." You don't have to make an exception in any way. People bring you what you want sometimes when you didn't know you wanted it. Accept happily.

If we don't always agree with each other, so be it. We can talk it over and try to understand each other's perspective. I can see her point, and she can see mine—and if we don't get together on it, well, I'm not the last person she'll know, and she's not the only person I'll ever know. We can get along.

So many people have helped me, and continue to. So many times, I call Betty Miller, who doesn't live at Judson. She's special. And there are many others here, some of whom are gone now. So many good things and so many good friends: if I don't have what they think I ought to, they bring it to me.

I have a great-grandson who's two now. When his parents brought him here to visit last year, we all went outside where there is play equipment. There was a hose running, and with his parents there, he started letting the water spray and pool around his feet. I looked at him but didn't say anything. If I had been the parent, I would have said, "I wouldn't do that, Honey, you might take a cold or you might fall down."

His parents didn't do anything or say anything. But he didn't get sick.

I thought, "Well, maybe the old ways are not necessarily the right ways now." I don't impose my views.

One of the keys to successful aging is taking things under advisement, but then ultimately making your own decision. Independent thinking is the key to freshness of thought and consideration. My much younger friend Kathryn Karipides says that at age 105 I am the most contemporary of her friends.

Here at Judson there are assisted living units, and then there's the high-rise, where I first lived. One or two other sections are all about the elderly, with additional care given, as in a convalescent home. The administration often has younger people come in to interact with us because they want us to see how young people can respond to us, and how we will respond to them. There are so many activities. They bring in lecturers. They bring in musicians. They bring in people who know the law. When you look over the schedule for the day, there is so much going on that no one can just sit and say, "I haven't got anything to do." But they don't tell you, you *have* to go.

I remember once Denise, the head nurse, came and

told me about a musical program that was going on. When she described the concert, I asked why I should go. She said because the musicians had gone out of their way to come and be with us that day.

I said, "I didn't invite them." The truth was, I just wasn't interested.

I didn't say that to be mean. I just wanted her to know that there were times when I actually might prefer sitting and reading a book, or I might need a nap, because I don't sleep well at night. Betty might drop in. If there is someone here I need to work with more than Betty, I might say, "Betty, will you excuse us? We'll get together another time."

Not "Go home, Betty" but "Will you?" That's the thing.

Another key to what you might call successful aging is celebrating the things that deserve it.

One of my teachers once told me that because my thoughts come faster than my words, they don't always wind up together. So now I write things down to address a gathering.

On my ninetieth birthday I wrote: "For years I responded to the question 'How old are you?' as many women do, with a sly grin or a figure everyone knows is much below the actual age. But after I passed three score and ten, and then another ten, it seemed to me a denial of God's gift of more years and my obligation to use them in ways helpful to others. Viewing them as a personal gift to use as I wished, I began to acknowledge, embrace, and celebrate them. The next step was to use them for others—encouraging, sympathizing, praying for and with those who wished it, smiling, hugging, and whatever else enhanced their well-being. To my surprise, these gestures began enhancing my own well-being— what a blessing!"

In 2001, at the age of ninety-seven, I moved to Judson's Gardenview Assisted Living Unit, where I functioned independently until 2006, when I was confined to a wheelchair due to arthritis in the knees. Recently I've been having pain in my shoulder, and when I turn, it hurts. I'm having therapy, which helps. But I don't jump around anymore: I move slowly. I have to accommodate myself the safest way I can.

My daughter-in-law Sandy says: "As Mom has grown older, I have never known her to make her family members accept responsibility for decisions regarding her care. With each progression to the next level of care at Judson Park, she has made the necessary arrangements prior to telling us that this is what she has decided to do.

"Moving from her apartment to extended care was extremely difficult for Mom. It not only meant relinquishing almost all of her independence, but also divesting herself of most of her worldly belongings—and all of the memorabilia from a long, challenging, and interesting life. When Paul and I came from Atlanta to help Mom make the move from her two-bedroom apartment to a one-bedroom in the assisted living unit, I was awed by the grace and strength she showed. She made no complaint nor shed any tears while the possessions of a lifetime were picked over and disposed of. I only knew how stressful it was because I saw it in her eyes when she admitted, 'Yes, dear, it is a bit overwhelming and I am a bit tired! I believe I will take a short nap.'"

The chair limits only the movements of my body, not my active mind. I read and I do crossword puzzles. I stay current with world events. I read *The 9-11 Commission Report* and a book called *Confessions of an Economic Hit Man*. People don't always know what older people can accomplish. They make assumptions.

Once, when I was eighty-nine, I had to go to the hospital emergency room during the Christmas season due to an asthma attack. I received the proper care. After about four hours, the doctor asked me if I was "online." I had to ask what he meant. Now I know he meant on the computer network.

The clincher was from the nurse, who asked, "Are you on the program?" I was sure I could answer her question if only I understood it—so I asked. Her answer was three more questions, including did I know what day it was, what year it was, and the name of the then president?

I burst out laughing and said, "Oh my Lord, of course I know all three."

At age eighty-nine I guess I shouldn't have been surprised that medical professionals would question the mental capacity of their patients; I'd never felt mine could be suspect. But I suppose it could.

When I have a medical issue to be resolved, I take the traditional remedies—nothing exotic. But I never think, "Oh, why bother at my age?" I don't believe in miracle remedies. I have a living will that stipulates that no extreme measures be taken should things come to that.

One thing that does anger me is the waste I've seen with Medicare, waste we need to rein in. Once after I was hospitalized for an operation, a doctor came by and literally looked at me from the doorway; he wasn't my regular doctor. Later when he sent a bill for a hospital visit, I asked why, and was told: "Why should you care? You're not the one who pays."

But we all pay when the system is this shamefully off-kilter from the real care given. Even fairly well-off people could get stuck with costs beyond their means. I believe everyone in the country deserves some kind of coverage.

When I was interviewed for my hundredth birthday, my black wheelchair barely contained my energy, Regina Brett wrote in the *Cleveland Plain Dealer*. She looked at all the books in my room and noted in particular the large dictionary sitting open so that I can look up any words I don't know. I told her about my birthday parties. I invite people for two reasons: I like them and I want them there. But I make it known to everyone through Betty and others who are planning the party that guests don't need to bring a gift to me.

I tell them I'm a beggar for needy people. When I was a hundred years old, I asked the two hundred people who came to Mt. Zion to help me celebrate to give money for people in Africa with HIV/AIDS. There was another gift in Kenya I made myself, and Mt. Zion responded, too. On that birthday, January 13, 2004, we raised three thousand dollars—in the middle of a blizzard! Instead of party favors we gave guests a list of my favorite books as well as a copy of *The Good Samaritan* painting I'd done in 1924 as a student at Fisk.

My daughter-in-law Mary Grace Concannon, Jim's wife, wrote to me later, "Your approach to your 100th birthday celebration was so like you: practical, problem-solving, logical, efficient, thoughtful, and clever."

For the 105th celebration, we received donations for two thousand dollars for Smile Train, which works on a matching-funds basis. The charity helps children with cleft palates get operations to alter their appearance. I've received pictures of one or two of the children. A single surgery costs $250, so we must have helped a number.

We all need a smile, and sometimes a soft touch—others who are willing to say, "I understand, and I'm willing to help." There are still things that need to be done, and I hope now, and when I'm gone, there will be ways people coming along will figure out, "I can help; this child doesn't need to starve; this child doesn't need to have a cleft tongue."

Oh yes, I begged. If you were my friend, and you came to my party, and you'd been told you didn't need to give me anything, I begged you to give it to the children instead.

CHAPTER EIGHT

WHAT PRICE FREEDOM?

Believe in life! Always human beings
will live and progress to greater, broader, and fuller life.

—W. E. B. Du Bois

"Despite reports of bone-chilling weather, unprecedented crowds, and tight security, the 105-year-old traveled to Washington, D.C., to witness history as the United States of America inaugurated its first African-American President, Barack Obama."

So said the bulletin put out by Judson Smart Living in 2009, the year our forty-fourth president was sworn in. I am quoted: "I want my children, my grandchildren, my great-grandchildren, to be able to say she was there." So I did.

In the interviews in local and national papers and on TV, they said I was a "trailblazer." But I've always believed that the struggle *is* the goal, as Dr. Martin Luther King stated it. Use your mind and goodwill. I don't believe in reparations, for the same reason I don't believe in "giving back," as in squaring an equation. Acting with compassion is its own reward.

On election night I wouldn't allow myself to fall asleep and listened eagerly to Obama's victory speech in which he referred to a woman like me, born a generation past slavery, when there were no cars, no planes, and no chance for black people—or women—to vote. I first took notice of Barack Obama when he spoke at the Democratic Convention in 2004. He struck me as sensible, interesting, and brilliant—different from many of the politicians of the past. During the campaign, I worried for his physical safety.

I read both of his autobiographical books with particular interest in his Kenyan background. I was inspired not only by his politics, but also by the love and dedication Barack Obama and his wife show their family—his concern for the children, and not just his. He seemed to care that all people take time for their children, at a time when so many children don't have fathers in their homes or in their lives.

When I saw his concern, I thought, "This is the man I want for president." We need to care for each other. Fortunately, in the time he's been in office, he's made proposals that would help people, including the children, the sick, and the financially needy. I hoped the president would say, "This is what I propose, and this is what I will give my all to." I believe he's doing the best he can. Now we're seeing that there are even some Democratic leaders who have different ideas.

For the trip to Washington, Judson's public relations director, Rob Lucarelli, made all the arrangements through the offices of Ohio senator Sherrod Brown, for which I was humbled and grateful. Judson was convinced it was worthwhile to help someone go. They showed me a proposal of what they were trying to do. It's part of their philosophy about successful aging. When they asked if I was interested in going, of course I said yes. Sherrod Brown provided the tickets, and Judson underwrote the other expenses. The staff at Judson arranged for me to be accompanied by Iris Williams, an RN at Judson.

Iris Williams relates: "When we told Mrs. Johnson the risks of being out in twenty to thirty degree weather for possibly seven hours; the lack of food, water, and comfort facilities; the crowd; multiple security checks; restrictions on bringing large bags into the Capitol building area; and the long walk to our pick-up destination afterwards, she looked us in the eye and said, 'Now we know the problems.'"

Kathryn Karipides states: "I've learned so many lessons from Ella Mae, but perhaps the most profound is the one I learned on January 18, 2009, the morning the weather report read, 'Still cold, still snowy: today's high will be twenty-five, but by "real feel" standards, it'll be more like twelve with anticipated snowfall of several inches.' I was worried. But when I arrived at Judson around 11:00 a.m., Ella Mae exuded excitement while getting dressed and going over her checklist. It was clear that she was going to the inauguration and that was it! When you've faced a lifetime of barriers and hardships and found ways to overcome them with strength of mind, fortitude, courage, and commitment, you don't give up. This was something she had dreamed of but never expected to happen in her lifetime. She had set her goal and she wasn't going to allow anything to stop her. Lesson learned: Warrior trumps worrier."

While other seniors decided not to go, I weighed common sense with this once-in-a-lifetime opportunity. When people worried about what might happen, I simply said that if something befell me on the trip, well, "So be it."

I knew I'd have the best of care.

Betty Miller remembers: "We were planning Ella Mae's 105th birthday celebration when she got the word that she was going to the inauguration. After checking her closets, we made a list of things she'd need, including a down coat; two pairs of slacks; turtleneck sweaters to match the slacks; pajamas; warm underwear; leggings; a warm-up suit; scarves; mittens; and an 'Obama' knit cap. Iris bought hand and leg warmers for Ella Mae. We packed everything carefully, including a beautiful lime green jacket Ella Mae wound up wearing to be interviewed by Gwen Ifill of PBS. Everyone was caught up in the excitement of this historic moment. The Sunday before the inauguration, I went to see her off and took pictures of Ella Mae all bundled up in her wheelchair. After she kissed and hugged all her well-wishers, Judson Park vice-president Roy Call and his wife Barbara Cross drove Ella Mae to the airport, followed by Iris and her family in their car. It was quite a send-off."

Despite all Betty's worries about warding off the cold, we stayed toasty in a furnished apartment in the

Georgetown Retirement Assisted Living facility in D.C. Someone at Judson had contacted the staff in Georgetown and made arrangements. When Iris and I approached and entered, the head of the institution was there to greet us.

On the way to my room, a staff person said, "We are glad to have you." When I was at a meal one day, another staff member came up and said, "We are *so* happy you came." It wasn't just for me; it was the spirit of the occasion. Everything went well.

I got up on Inauguration Day hours before dawn and put on my pearls and then layers of clothes. What kept me warm for eight hours out on the Mall in Washington on Inauguration Day turned out to be a sleeping bag that Iris had borrowed from Roy Call, just in case. A picture of my mummylike self appeared in several newspapers. You can just see my glasses peering out from all the puffy layers. I have a coat, scarf, and hat on underneath it all.

As Iris Williams relates: "The courteous and curious crowd gave Mrs. Johnson the 'right-of-way.' It was like the parting of the Red Sea! A student interviewed her for a school project, and multigenerational families stopped to pose for pictures and share stories."

En route to the Mall, someone representing Gwen Ifill approached us. Later I was also interviewed by Joe Shapiro from National Public Radio in the car, which was difficult, because though it was large enough for a lot of people, it wasn't quite big enough for me to turn around in easily. I have some—what do they call them—disabilities. I don't rejoice in them. But we all did the best we could.

It was really moving to be out there on that lawn, despite the cold. There were many others who also deserved to go. On the plane I saw a man I'd known for years; I didn't know that he was once a member of the Tuskegee Airmen. I recognized him; one of my sons had known him and worked with him. Then another one came on with whom I'd served at a settlement house. He came over and said he was glad to see me. So one thing ran into another, and that's how we got there.

Iris Williams remembers praying every step of the way to the inauguration that nothing would go wrong: "Mrs. Johnson never complained. The only thing she ever asked me was to rub her nose after I had bundled her in the sleeping bag."

Though we still need change, we also need to celebrate how far we've come. It's been a long time since I had to pass for white in order to travel. My first husband,

Elmer, could pass, and did when he wanted to. At some point in our marriage, he went to North Carolina, and the train conductor said, "Make that nigger get up out of that seat," so that a white person could sit down.

Elmer said, "Oh no. Just let him sit."

He was not embarrassed to say that. He was making a point, that he could be accepted as a white person. The fact of the matter is that we're all mixed. But people of African descent have been called "black" for years.

I don't call myself white. I could pass sometimes, though. A lot of people did it. It was not necessarily honorable, but we had to get past a government that was keeping us down. So much has happened in America since the first Africans came as slaves. They had to find a way. I learned so much about the early days from Jubilee songs like "Go Tell It on the Mountain—Go Tell Old Pharaoh to Let My People Go."

Once when I was in my late thirties, I was going to Texas from Cleveland on a round-trip ticket my husband had bought. One of Elmer's coworkers who happened to be white went to make the purchase, because Elmer was not getting around easily at that point. So this colleague accommodated him. He had his own car, in which he and Elmer drove from place to place, especially those places that had to do with their jobs, because they worked in the same department.

On my way south, I had to change in St. Louis. Of course when I was leaving Cleveland, I was leaving a place where I didn't have to have a ticket designated for a white person or a colored person. I could go from here to Akron or to Chicago or wherever without a different ticket. But when I crossed the Mason-Dixon Line, I gave in my ticket to get on the train, and someone directed me to the regular car.

But when I presented the ticket, the conductor said, "You can't use this; you have to go in the other coach— that's where your people go."

I said, "But it's been paid for."

He said: "Just get in. We're about to leave. When you get in, we can straighten it out."

I got in, and eventually he came and he sat down, and in a very friendly, congenial way, he said, "Oh, you're going to Texas."

I said, "Yes."

"Do you know anyone in Texas?"

I said, "Yes, I grew up there."

That's when he showed what he was aiming at. He said, "You know, then, that you can't stay in the same car with whites."

I should have been on the one for "Colored"; that's the way he interpreted it. It was an overnight ride, and in the morning, I got up and went to the washroom. As it happened, a white woman was there and told the conductor she thought I was colored or Negro—whatever she called me. By that time Dallas was two hours away, so I let the conductor put me in the Colored car.

Another time I had gone to Louisiana and was on the way back to Cleveland. In the evening when I was leaving New Orleans, the porter saw my ticket. He said, "When you get on the train, get in the upper berth." This was a sleeper, too.

"You get on the upper, cover your face up, and in the morning put on some heavy makeup and some lipstick, and make sure to wear a cap. We'll make out like you're white."

I didn't object. I wanted to get home. I couldn't have solved the problem; that's the way it was then. Now there were people who fought, who lost their lives for the freedom to ride where they and others wanted on the trains. We don't cherish that for anyone.

In those days black and white were not to mix on the trains. Some of the laws that mandated segregation of the races made no sense. The way the trains were set up, there were two sets of seats facing each other, for four people, and on the opposite side was a seat for two.

We weren't getting what we were charged for. Because of the laws they were enforcing, if I sat on the smaller seat and friends took the one for four even if there weren't four of them, the white people would have to stand, because they couldn't mix with us. It was our way of trying to get what was being denied us. Seats were lost because the Jim Crow laws were designed to separate us. The people in charge weren't using common sense.

There were other rules and customs that were unfair and degrading and defied logic. In Cleveland there were certain things you were not supposed to do. If I wanted a hat, I could buy it, but I couldn't try it on. It was assumed that black people had dirt on them or something else that could be transferred, somehow. This type of practice went on all the way until the 1950s and even later.

And if you went to a restaurant, they didn't have to deny you publicly. They had other ways to make you uncomfortable. In fact, one of the members of my church and sorority went into Taylor's Tea Room once in the

1950s. The Tea Room was located in Taylor's Department Store in downtown Cleveland, which closed in 1961. My friend sat, and sat, and sat. Eventually she started a conversation with the waitress.

My friend asked, "Is it because I am colored that I couldn't get waited on before other people?"

The waitress said, "Yes." She admitted the truth as opposed to the "official" policy.

My friend could have taken them to court. Someone else I knew had crushed ice served in her food to make it unattractive. She sued the place and won. But the restaurant wasn't too concerned, because this was not an uncommon incident. The management had even put money aside to defend itself in these types of situations.

I knew some real activists, such as Zelma Watson George and her husband. Also trained as a social worker, an accomplished musician and composer, Zelma was multitalented, highly regarded, and a fellow member of Alpha Kappa Alpha. When I became acquainted with her, I discovered she was born about the middle of December, and I was born thirteen days into the next January. My time in Texas was in Dallas. Hers was in Hearn. Her parents were educated. I believe her father, Samuel Watson, trained for a teaching career; but after he got married, he decided he wasn't making enough, as his family grew to five daughters and a son, to stay in education. At that time the churches were beginning to pay the ministers more than the educators received. So he decided he could do better in the church. He was prepared, he was a good speaker, he was reliable—all the things we like in the pulpit. Zelma's father, Rev. Watson, became minister of the then biggest Baptist church in Dallas. It was there that the family started very strong activity in civil rights. Her father was an activist preacher. Du Bois and Booker T. Washington debated on the church's grounds. Marian Anderson sang in his church. Visitors to the family home included James Weldon Johnson and A. Philip Randolph. When they moved to Dallas, Zelma was in the twelfth grade. But she didn't go to a school, like I did. Her mother taught her at home. Zelma was the oldest child.

By the time Zelma decided she wanted to go to Chicago for college, the family had moved to Topeka, Kansas. Rev. Watson's activities on behalf of Negro prisoners he considered innocent had brought the family unwelcome attention from the Ku Klux Klan in Texas; so they went west.

Zelma was brilliant, and she had benefited from

exposure to the people from all over who came to visit the family, wherever they were. But when she got ready to go to the University of Chicago, where her father had friends on the faculty, she learned there was no dormitory for colored students. So her father said, "I'll find a place in Chicago; I will not have my child living with strangers." When there was an opening in a very big Baptist church there, he applied and got it.

Zelma was a big woman, and when I first met her, she was dressed in a plaid skirt and a sweater, with long pigtails. It was a schoolgirl kind of outfit. The members of AKA told her: "You are no little girl; this sorority is not for little girls. You have to get rid of those pigtails." She was in her twenties then.

She didn't fashion herself a civil rights leader in the mold of someone like Dr. Martin Luther King. She just lived her life. She always said her color was against her; although she looked white, she was treated as black. The other obstacle was her size; but she overcame all of it. Eventually Zelma got a PhD in sociology from NYU and received a Rockefeller Foundation grant to study African American music. She was a performer, too, singing the lead role in a production of Gian Carlo Menotti's *The Medium* at the opening of newly named Karamu Theater.

President Eisenhower sent her around the world as a goodwill ambassador. In 1960, she was appointed as an alternate to the U.S. delegation to the UN. On her most exciting day there, nine African nations were admitted.

Zelma George was a multitalented woman and a real leader in our beloved sisterhood. In addition, she was cochairman of the "Carl Stokes for Mayor" committee in 1967, helping elect Stokes as the first African American mayor of a major American city. In 1967, AKA honored her, and they used the occasion of a luncheon to raise money for the Job Corps center. I was cochairperson of the event. Since Carl Stokes had just been elected mayor, the sorority asked him to sit at the speakers' table. I was acting as mistress of ceremonies.

I was nervous, and stumbled on the words in my introductory remarks. Carl asked me, "Have you been drinking?"

I said, "No, it's too early." It was only lunchtime! Carl didn't recognize me, because when I helped his mother when he was a little boy, I was known to him as Mrs. Cheeks.

Zelma and her attorney husband, Claybourne George, were known for their festive gatherings. There were those in town who resented Zelma; as a widower,

Claybourne was a good catch. His wife Enola, who'd been active in AKA, had passed away. Some people were jealous of the attention Zelma got for being with Claybourne as well as for her own accomplishments.

As a couple, they got around town. Sometimes when he came home, Zelma's husband would challenge her and say: "Want to have some fun? Let's go where they don't want us. Some of these merchants have put money aside to be used if they lose in court, and if we go and they lose in court, we'll get some money."

This may not have been the most admirable technique. The point was that they wouldn't have behaved as they did, except that they felt they were being abused. We found ways. You know, you don't *have* to fight, as Martin Luther King said; you don't need to be nasty. You don't need to knock someone down. You use your mind and your goodwill. But you need to be sensible with it. That's Obama's approach, too. His rhetoric is inclusive, not confrontational.

I don't know if I'm an oddity or not. I don't want to be. But I want to think, if I am wrong, let's talk about it. If there's something between the two of us, or if you're angry with me, I don't say, "Get thee away."

I say, "Let's get together."

CHAPTER NINE

EMANCIPATION PROCLAMATION

We must accept finite disappointment,
but never lose infinite hope.

—MARTIN LUTHER KING JR.

We have to forget what we did before, what we believed before, in order to move on as a country and as a world. That was then; this is now.

I don't believe it's necessary to get approval. I want approval. I sincerely do. I just feel that we ought to be able to get it allowing you and you and you to say what you think. What I need—what we all need—most is not necessarily love or approval but respect. We don't necessarily need to love each other: Scripture may say so, but many of us don't pay attention to Scripture until we can use it to prove a point.

If someone says, "Ella Mae, I think you ought to do this," and it belittles me, I won't go along. God gave me a brain, too. I don't say that to be clever or to belittle anyone else. But if something is important, I want it to be right. I do not claim to know it all. I'm not saying you and the others don't know. I'm saying, "Let's talk," and see where we end up.

I want to know enough so that if a decision is right, great—and if it isn't, change it. I don't hesitate to change. But I want to know what the effect is going to be. Sometimes I can't. If a change brings an effect I hadn't anticipated, I say, "Well, adjust to that."

At the time of the American Revolution, Patrick Henry said: "Peace? There is no peace." That has stayed with many people, because if you accepted the U.S. Constitution and the Emancipation Proclamation, there would be no peace until there was equality. Abraham Lincoln didn't speak just because he wanted to speak; he included everyone. We're all free. Nobody is above me. I am not above anyone. We are equal. The Emancipation Proclamation was not the beginning of all this: the Declaration of Independence was. We won our independence from England. Later on, when there were people who felt differently about it, the tumult started.

I did not travel with Dr. Martin Luther King, but I did attend services at which he spoke, at Antioch Baptist Church here in Cleveland in the 1960s. He came to town during Carl Stokes's bid to become mayor. I wouldn't say

Dr. King came to support Carl specifically, but once he was here, he did. I don't claim that I ever achieved anything in terms of advancing the civil rights cause: I wasn't trying to. I was just a part of a group that needed to understand where we are—not just where we are, but where the country is.

I never knew Rosa Parks, but I followed her actions, and I agreed with them. When she didn't get up to let a white man be seated, someone suggested, "Why didn't she say, 'I did this because I was tired'?"

Someone else added, "She might have said, 'tired of what's going on.'" She wasn't saying she was physically tired. She was just tired of having people tell her she had to get up. She'd had enough.

When King referred to the Emancipation Proclamation, it had to do with my race. Dr. King's message was "Don't hate other people, don't hate white people; some of them are here with us. We've needed them and still do." Though Gandhi was dead by then, King had absorbed his message. So much of what is important is not necessarily what happens today; but what happens today needs to be seen in light of what happened yesterday. What happens today might be, "I need a dollar." What happened yesterday might have been, "I didn't need a dollar, or material things—I needed love. I needed someone to pat me on the shoulder, or say hello, and make me feel like I'm somebody." They don't have to be important—just someone who stops long enough to acknowledge you.

All of us must remember that Dr. King's ideas followed some of the nation's proclamations of what we want, or what we as a country need. He stressed that the key is to work with people, not to order them around. A lot of the people who fought the civil rights movement also opposed the work of whites—of Quakers and others who stood up against the treatment of the slaves, but still didn't want to take anything away from other people.

I don't think Patrick Henry was thinking of black or white when he said "Peace? There is no peace." He was referring to the strictures the American colonists were living with under British rule.

I think of the Japanese who came to the United States and were taken from their homes and schools and churches and moved into special settlements once we went to war with Japan in the Second World War. Certainly, there was no peace for them, with the government questioning their allegiance. Unless they have taken my money or my opportunities, I want them to have what I have. And I want to do what I can to support my family. I was a widow. I didn't have to have assistance. I never asked for assistance. There were things that came to me, just as there are things that come to me now. But I wanted, as much as possible, for them to come the right way.

I feel that if we don't have equality yet, we should fight for it even *now*. I didn't appreciate that there were people who could afford to provide for others and they didn't. But I don't expect people to follow my line of thinking—they are not obligated. They want to be free to make their own choices. I believe that this is what the national government started out with but didn't follow through on—that every man is free and equal. We know that. But that's what I take as representing the government's role—to work with people, not order them.

I am no better than you, but I am certainly no worse. I don't want people to decide what they want based only on what I might decide: I never fought for that. I did fight for a chance, and if I don't use it, that's my fault. I suppose to some extent I did think I felt I was a bit different as a descendent of slaves. But I don't believe in reparations.

If I want to engage a younger person, or someone who might not share all my views, I might just say: "Hello!

That looks interesting. What do you think about it?" I wouldn't press my point, because that is taking away the other person's freedom to form his or her opinion. Freedom to make up your own mind, whether it's about religion or politics or what you want for supper that night, is the ultimate freedom. In dealing with others who may not agree with you, the idea is to encourage conversation and discussion.

Don't be taken advantage of; but don't take advantage of others, either. My way is to ask questions, and move slowly. Take things gradually. Don't try to turn the world upside down overnight. In time, you can find success, unless you go in thinking: "It ought to be mine, I should have it; I shouldn't have to fight for it." An entitled attitude won't get you far.

No one has absolute authority. Freedom also means free to live each day as I see fit. Nobody owes me anything, not even God. I've had a good life. I've been blessed over and over. I've had a magnificent journey. I accept the good with the difficult.

Here's what I learned all those years ago from Tennie Davis: I'm convinced that had she been asked what she wanted for me, it would *not* have been, "I want her to be happy." She would have wanted me to achieve goals I set for myself, knowing I would be happy as a result of my own efforts. Nor would she have said, "I want life to be easier for her than it was for me." I'm sure she would think that whatever challenges I overcame would strengthen me, and so I should not be denied the experience.

Values imparted in my early years have stayed with me all these years; I cannot say it to her directly but I state it now: "I attribute to you, Mama, most, if not all, that is good within me." I pray regularly that I will be as compassionate as Mama was.

I'm alone but I'm not lonely. I have something to read or write, or something I want to think about. I don't just sit at home. There are people who call me. Sometimes I'm busy. People may drop in and want me to play hostess. I'm thinking, "As soon as he or she leaves, I can go back to sleep!"

I don't need anyone to come to keep me happy. In fact, I didn't like it when I had relatives by marriage that would just drop in. I might be planning to write a letter. I might want to sit and think, "What do I do tomorrow?"

If someone just drops in, I can't make my own decision. If I were coming to you, I would call you and say: "Hi, I am not busy. Is it all right for me to come and see you?" I would give him or her a chance to say, "Well, I can't do it right now."

If people want to see me, they can call and make an appointment. If that sounds cold, well, I'm sorry. I shouldn't say, "Sorry." I say, "Well, that's unfortunate." I'm not sorry. I'm not telling the truth if I say, "I'm sorry." That doesn't mean I always tell the truth.

I might say to you, "Come over; I'd like to have you come." I would welcome you, but I might be tired, or I might be thinking, "I should be doing something else now." But I wouldn't say that, which is why I wouldn't be telling the whole truth.

When someone comes by, I need to be dressed. I want to look nice.

Sometimes we need to make compromises, when you are unable to do anything about the situation. I would never tell someone, "Oh no, you don't come." I'd say, "Can we do it another day?"

I guess that's Ella Mae. That's me—I don't change. I don't expect anyone to plan for me to change. I handle things my way.

CHAPTER TEN

LESSONS FOR
MY GRANDCHILDREN

Sometimes a single word will lift the spirit.

And sometimes it is destined that one must only listen.

Sometimes a smile will bridge the empty darkness.

Sometimes just nearness is the answer.

—WINSTON O. ABBOTT

Step-by-step, actions taken on my behalf by individuals, groups, and institutions have made me who I am today. All my life I have sought to respond to Jesus' "If you love me, feed my sheep." I have a copy of the painting of *The Good Samaritan* on my dresser, and I look at it as I fall asleep at night and again when I awake in the morning.

In the beginning, when I had been chosen by the Davises so many years before, and they had done so much for me, I felt, "They are helping me, and I need it." I didn't just need material things, but other things, some of which Mrs. Davis gave. The most important was acceptance without question.

Good Samaritans gave me the love and guidance I needed early in life—and they have guided me since in all my endeavors. I know that being a Good Samaritan has contributed to my longevity. Compassion is the key to the good life—help without expecting a payback. And helping is not necessarily about finances.

As I said in my acceptance speech for the Judson Smart Living Award in 2009: "These many years have allowed me the opportunity to practice and practice some more and to learn from my errors. Maybe one of these days I'll really get it right. Through all these years, I have kept my faith, my convictions, and my interest in the people of the world. And I have kept my hope, always my hope for change, for a better and more equitable world for all people."

The most important lesson I've learned over the course of a lifetime: not just surviving, or getting along, but being useful. Too often we remember, "Ask and ye shall receive; seek and ye shall find," and we believe all we have to do is ask. When we don't get the response we seek right away, we think our prayer has gone unanswered. Patience is essential. Heaven is always here, within us, if we have the patience to discover it. Sometimes we pray for things that we aren't, in fact, supposed to get—things that are bad for us. Maybe "no answer" means we need more time to discover that answer on our own, or to find out that another choice is possible. Not having a prayer answered right away doesn't mean He doesn't care; maybe He thinks this is just not the time. Maybe there's something else in the future that will help. Compassion is patient in its essence. As it says in Psalm 27, "Wait on the Lord: Be of good courage, and He shall strengthen thine heart."

Moderation is also a key element for me: I've never needed a lot to be satisfied. I could find in people and in circumstances, things that mattered to me. I think they've kept me, well, fulfilled. I feel I've done well if I've done the right thing. It is impossible to put value on the great satisfaction derived from thinking of others and trying to help them.

I like to think that I've passed on these lessons to my grandchildren and great-grandchildren. The long talks I've had with all of them have shown me the differences between the generations, not only because of the intervening years but also because of the revolution in expectations, aspirations, and responsibilities.

I still have a way to go but my hopes were raised when my grandson George told me, "We don't agree, Grandma, but you listen." I took great joy in encouraging all my grandchildren in what they wanted to do.

George Cheeks remembers: "When I was much younger, I was very active in community theater in Cleveland. At the age of twelve, I decided I wanted to adapt, direct, star in, and produce a production of the musical *You're a Good Man Charlie Brown*, which would travel to elementary schools, hospitals, and nursing homes throughout Cleveland. It was quite a daunting task for a twelve-year-old, but I was determined. The first venue that accepted our request to perform was Judson Park. Right before the lights dimmed and the show was about to begin, nervously I took a quick peek at the audience. The first thing that caught my eye was my grandmother and her close friends sitting dead center. She was beaming and excited and it motivated me to do the best I could, so I could make her proud. My grandma's approval was more important to me than I ever wanted to admit."

I always tried to support my grandchildren, even if I didn't see their choices as something I would have suggested myself.

During annual visits to the home of granddaughter Audrey and her family, I spent a lot of time with Audrey's daughter, Nika. Even at the age of three, she helped me bake cookies and rolls. One evening after dinner when she was four and in nursery school, I told her I was going to our room to do some knitting. She came with her "homework." Eventually we ceased talking and I hope I never forget the quiet, serenity, and connectedness I felt with her then. We had a real bond that continues to this day.

Here's some of what Nika wrote on her application to the University of Southern California at Santa Barbara, from which she graduated in 2006:

"I count one, two, three, four—no, just a piece of lint—five, six grapefruit seeds in this lavender-scented envelope. As tradition states, I take out six pennies to match my great-grandmother's number of grapefruit seeds.

"Since I was old enough to reach the drawer of my father's desk that I knew safeguarded his office supplies from my dirty, goo-covered fingers, I have been exchanging grapefruit seeds for pennies with my great-grandmother. When we began our secret trading, I saw it as nothing more than a game. Once my handwriting finally progressed to a legible stage, my great-grandmother and I were able to trade words. As the exchange of ideas began, our secret connection became more than a childish delight. Though the envelopes are now in a different desk, and my hands are now washed and even moisturized, our 'exchange' still exists.

"It is not the dry and shriveled grapefruit seeds that hold any real value. Instead it is the occasional note permeated by my great-grandmother's lavender-scented perfume, or the photographs faded by time that accompanied those grapefruit seeds, that truly establishes the relationship between my great-grandmother and me. From this exchange of pictures, ideas, and memories, I have learned a great deal from her. Her never-ending supply of stories has enabled me to see her not as a woman at the end of her days, nearly a foot shorter than me, with frizzy white hair, but as a teacher.

"Through her, I have lived through the Great War. I have survived the Great Depression and been through just about everything else in the last century. All the impersonal memories and documentaries I've seen could never replace the true narratives I have 'shared' with my great-grandmother. Not only has she taught me more about the world than any teacher; she has also forced me to make changes in my life.

"Though I have always been a disciplined student—which can be seen as I line up my glistening pennies in a perfectly straight line—my great-grandmother has taught me what it means to truly persevere. As an African-American widow in the early twentieth century, she faced discrimination, financial difficulties, and succeeded in raising two sons alone. Her inner strength makes all my teenage trials seem completely trivial. My great-grandmother's hard work and infinite perseverance have changed my attitudes towards life. With her as my conscience, I can no longer take the easy way out or pity myself for my inconsequential troubles. Through her I have been able to see how much inner strength it takes to survive in this world.

"Once I was old enough to understand the stories of Mrs. Ella Mae Johnson, I realized the risk of judging a book by its cover. I've learned from her that once you can look past the biases and stereotypes attached to others, you will open yourself up to people with rich and varied stories to tell who are just waiting for someone to listen."

I was also touched by a letter I received from an anonymous staff member at Judson after I got back from the inauguration.

"Since knowing you," she told me in her note, "I have learned that the struggle for social justice is ongoing, with the rewards often incremental and seemingly insignificant. But if I continue to plant the seeds, some-day someone will reap a bountiful harvest from my efforts. It is the seed-planting that is important—that we pass along and inspire others towards the struggle."

After I got home from the inauguration in Washington, I thought about the fact that we will have real change in this country only if all citizens make it happen, not just the man at the top. As the president said that day, the real story is *hope* for all humanity, regardless of race or religious preference. I can think of nothing more inspiring for the world than all of us, together, striving for peace, prosperity, and justice for all.

I think our president came into office hoping and believing there were enough people who wanted what he wanted that he would have no problem. But we see that he does have a problem from some of the people who were backing him before, depending on their politics. Even some of us differ. People in Washington started thinking of how they had to account to their constituencies.

When the president and his wife had an opportunity to expose themselves and their children to the public, I thought, "How wonderful."

I still think, "How wonderful." But he was mistaken

in thinking everyone else shares my view. I think now he realizes that his hope was not attainable so easily, and he didn't take into consideration just how important money was in all that he hopes to achieve. I don't blame him. I just say that he really didn't know how much he had to do to fight for what is good and right.

My hope for him is my hope for the country. If he fails, we all do. He knows this when he says, "Not me, but you. Not us, but all of us."

We are in it together.

What's important for me now is the same thing that it always was—compassion. I can't think of anything more important. I've loved my fellow citizens. I've loved my children. I'm happy with the opportunity that I've had to worship the way I want to worship. I'm not worshiping somebody else's God, but I am insisting on the ability to worship my way, and be the person He would have me be.

I hope I am remembered as one who helped others when they needed it. And I hope the people who love me will carry on that legacy, doing what's best for all of us, not just you and yours.

ELLA MAE'S AWARDS

1978   The Phillis Wheatley Association Recognition of
        Faithful and Tireless Service, presented by
        Phillis Wheatley Association

1983   "Continued Support" Award, presented by
        Junior League of Mt. Zion Congregational
        Church

1991   The Creative Craft Club of Mt. Zion
        Congregational Church

2003   Seventy-five Dear Member of Alpha Kappa
        Alpha Sorority, Inc.

2004   Centurion Fiskite, Class of 1925, awarded by
Cleveland Fisk Club

2004   Proclamation on her 100th Birthday from the
Honorable Louis Stokes, Congressman (retired)

2004   Proclamation on her 100th Birthday from
Alpha Omega Chapter of Alpha Kappa Alpha
Sorority, Inc.

2004   Proclamation on her 100th Birthday from
Mt. Zion Congregational Church, United
Church of Christ

2004   Proclamation on her 100th Birthday from
the Honorable Stephanie Tubbs Jones,
Congresswoman (dec.)

2004   Proclamation on her 100th Birthday from Bob
Taft, Governor, State of Ohio

2004   Proclamation on her 100th Birthday from the
Honorable Jane L. Campbell, Mayor

2004   Resolution of Congratulations on her 100th
Birthday from the City of Cleveland, City
Council President, Frank Jackson

2004   Proclamation on her 100th Birthday from the
       Ohio House of Representatives

2005   Distinguished Alumni Award, Mandel School of
       Applied Social Sciences, Case Western Reserve
       University

2006   Highest Service Award, Alpha Kappa Alpha
       Sorority, Inc.

2007   Cleveland mayor Frank Jackson issues citywide
       proclamation in honor of her 103rd birthday

2008   Honored as Case Western Reserve's oldest living
       African American alumna

2009   Cleveland mayor Frank Jackson issues citywide
       proclamation in honor of her 105th Birthday

2009   Proclamation on her 105th Birthday from the
       Honorable Marcia L. Fudge, Congresswoman

2009   United States Senate Certificate of Special
       Recognition in honor of her 105th Birthday by
       Sherrod Brown, U.S. Senator

2009   Judson Smart Living Award

ELLA MAE'S FAVORITE BOOKS

The Bible

Come Walk Among the Stars, Winston O. Abbott

Tuesdays with Morrie, Mitch Albom

The Heart of a Woman, Maya Angelou

Days of Grace, Arthur Ashe

Dear and Glorious Physician, Taylor Caldwell

Great Lion of God, Taylor Caldwell

I, Judas, Taylor Caldwell

The Blood of Abraham: Insights into the Middle East,
  Jimmy Carter

Sources of Strength: Meditations on Scripture for a Living Faith, Jimmy Carter

God's Name in Vain: The Wrongs and Rights of Religion in Politics, Stephen L. Carter

Wealth Creation for Small Business Owners, James E. Cheeks, Esq.

My Life, Bill Clinton

It Takes a Village, Hillary Rodham Clinton

Guide My Feet: Prayers and Meditations for Our Children, Marian Wright Edelman

The Good Book: Reading the Bible with Mind and Heart, Peter J. Gomes

Sermons: Biblical Wisdom for Daily Living, Peter J. Gomes

God in Search of Man: A Philosophy of Judaism, Abraham Joshua Heschel

I Asked for Wonder: A Spiritual Anthology, Abraham Joshua Heschel

Stride Toward Freedom, Dr. Martin Luther King Jr.

When Bad Things Happen to Good People, Rabbi
    Harold S. Kushner

Who Needs God, Rabbi Harold S. Kushner

W. E. B. Du Bois: Biography of a Race, David L. Lewis

*Dreams from My Father: A Story of Race and
    Inheritance*, Barack Obama

*The Audacity of Hope: Thoughts on Reclaiming the
    American Dream*, Barack Obama

Come with Me to the Holy Land, Harriet-Louise H.
    Patterson

*And They Shall Be My People: An American Rabbi and
    His Congregation*, Paul Wilkes